God's Lamp, Man's Light

---

*Mysteries
of the
Menorah*

Restoration Foundation

Understanding the Jewish roots of our faith is a golden key that unlocks the treasures of Holy Scripture and enriches our Christian lives. This concept is the focus of Restoration Foundation, an international, transdenominational, multicultural publishing and educational resource to the body of Christ

Restoration Foundation features a network of scholars, church leaders, and laypersons who share the vision for restoring the Hebrew foundations of Christian faith and returning the church to a biblical relationship of loving support for the international Jewish community and the nation of Israel.

We are pleased to make available to all denominations and fellowships the teaching of the gifted scholars and Christian leaders in our network. Conferences, seminars, and other instructional forums are available on a wide range of topics that can be tailored to each individual setting. These concepts are taught throughout the world in our International Institutes.

We publish *Restore!* magazine, a high-quality journal featuring theological balance and scholarly documentation, that helps Christians recover their Hebrew heritage while strengthening their faith in Jesus.

Restoration Foundation also publishes and distributes Golden Key Books in order to disseminate teaching about Christianity's Judaic foundations. The Living Emblems Series is a division of Golden Key Books that offers solid instruction on various biblical symbols, artifacts, and practices that the Jewish people and the church have used to illustrate biblical truths in remembrance of God's mighty acts of history. Living Emblems also makes these items of Judaica available for purchase.

The ministry of Restoration Foundation is made possible by our many partners around the world who share in our Golden Key Partnership program. We invite you to join us in sharing the satisfaction of knowing that you are a partner in an organization that is making a difference in the world by restoring Christians to their biblical Hebrew heritage, by eradicating Judaeophobia and anti-Semitism, by supporting Israel and the international Jewish community, and by encouraging collaborative efforts among those who share this vision.

For information about Restoration Foundation, *Restore!* magazine, Golden Key Books, Living Emblems, and Golden Key Partnerships, contact us at the address below.

Restoration Foundation
P. O. Box 421218
Atlanta, Georgia 30342, U.S.A.
www.RestorationFoundation.org

God's Lamp, Man's Light

*Mysteries
of
the Menorah*

John D. Garr, Ph.D., Th.D.

GOLDEN KEY BOOKS

Living Emblems Series

Restoration Foundation
P. O. Box 421218
Atlanta, Georgia 30342, U.S.A.

To Richard and Dawn Rawson and my colleagues, the leaders of the Houston-based Association of Jewish and Christian Believers who have encouraged and faithfully supported this publishing ministry.

TABLE OF CONTENTS

Preface

The menorah is *the* biblical symbol *par excellence*. The graceful symmetry of its flowing lines displays a profound beauty that is soothing, reassuring, and uplifting to the human spirit. Esthetically appealing, it is an attractive decoration for any home or sanctuary. At the same time, however, the menorah evokes powerful images of the Divine, assuring its observer that it is far more than an *objet d'art*. This is a heavenly symbol that transcends the imagination of earthly artisans.

Originally designed as the means of providing light in the holy place of the Israelites' wilderness sanctuary, the menorah has become more symbol than apparatus to the Jewish people. It has come to represent the presence of God among his people, the Eternal Light who illuminates his chosen and through them enlightens the world. When, after a nineteen-century hiatus, the nation of Israel was restored, the modern Israelis chose the menorah as the dominant symbol to grace the reborn state's national seal, a testimony to its enduring importance in the corporate Jewish consciousness. The ancient menorah still speaks to Israel of the undying and irresistible force of light.

A Lost Legacy

Unfortunately, most Christians have not recognized the powerful imagery manifest in the menorah. Relegated in Christian understanding to the status of an implement in the ancient tabernacle, it has been regarded by those Christians with knowledge of its existence as an archaic device, a material artifact that was totally replaced by the symbolism of Christian faith. Though the church has continued to use candlesticks of various designs in its sanctuaries, the menorah has been generally disregarded. It has, therefore, had little significance for most Christians.

A major factor in Christianity's ignorance of the menorah has been its lack of prominence in the New Testament. Except for an oblique reference in the Apocalypse to seven golden lampstands, the menorah is unmentioned in the Apostolic Writings. The church's focus on the New Testament to the neglect and occasionally even to the exclusion of the Hebrew Scriptures has left Christian leaders and laity largely ignorant of the purely biblical, Hebraic symbols, among which the menorah stands paramount. Not only have Christians been robbed of the beauty of the menorah's display in sanctuaries and homes, but they have also been denied understanding of the rich symbolism manifest in its design.

Christianity's continuing unawareness of the rich menorah tradition has also been exacerbated by the rabbinic prohibition against constructing replicas of the appliances in the temple after its destruction in 70 C.E. In an effort to ensure that those devices would not be corrupted and/or used for purposes other than their designed intent, the rabbinic council legislated against replication of any of the implements of temple worship, including the seven-branched menorah. A menorah of five or eight branches could be fabricated; however, the construction of a seven-branched menorah was forbidden.

The Jews understood the need for this prohibition, for they fully believed that the temple would be restored. They were able to maintain their menorah consciousness by its detailed description both in the Hebrew Scriptures and in the oral tradition of the sages and by the use of its substitute, the eternal lamp in their synagogues. Christians, however, were not exposed to menorahs even in Jewish synagogues, homes, and businesses because this injunction precluded their construction and display. Except for a carved image of the menorah on the Arch of Titus in Rome, there was no visualization of the menorah that was accessible to Christians. Even if they happened to read the biblical text describing the menorah, they were left to imagine what appearance it may have taken.

Stripped of its biblical legacy, its heritage with and among the Jewish people, Christianity has been impoverished, severed from the Jewish roots of its faith and from their rich, nourishing sap. This fact has been further exacerbated by nineteen centuries of ecclesiastical Judaeophobia, anti-Judaism, and anti-Semitism. In a rush to define itself apart from Jews and Judaism, the post-Nicene and medieval church distanced itself from a profound portion of its Judaic heritage. Biblical festivals were replaced by holy days of often questionable origin. Biblical norms of community and congregation were replaced by politico-ecclesiastical systems patterned after secular empires. Jewish tradition was replaced by church tradition. Biblically Hebraic symbols were replaced by "Christian" symbols.

TIME FOR RESTORATION

After centuries of darkness concerning the deep Hebraic roots of Christian faith, the church is experiencing a revival of interest in things Jewish. Believers of virtually every ethnicity and denomination are rediscovering the long-lost legacy of Christianity's Jewish connection. Biblical truths and practices long buried under the rubble of human tradition are being resurrected by those who have determined in their hearts "to do God's thing God's way."

Among these renewals is the return to biblical symbols and to understanding the person and work of Jesus Christ and the ministry of the church that are readily manifest in these ancient emblems of living faith. A growing trend of Hebraic restoration is sweeping the Christian landscape, a trend that will only increase exponentially as more Christians are prompted by the Holy Spirit to embrace the Hebraic truths that are foundational to their faith.

This book is part of the Golden Key Books *Living Emblems Series*, materials designed to help Christians discover the importance of the biblically Hebraic symbols. In it, you will see the solid biblical background of the menorah, both in the Old and New Testaments. You will be assisted in understanding the menorah tradition of the sages of Israel. You will also share in the rich paradigms of light and life among the Jewish people. Finally, you will understand more than ever before the person and work of Jesus, the Messiah, the living Menorah, the light of the world. You will simply be amazed at the mysteries of divine understanding that are clearly revealed in God's lamp, man's light.

I am most grateful to Dr. Charles Bryant-Abraham and Judy Grehan for their careful critique of the manuscript and for their excellent suggestions regarding content. I am also indebted to friends and colleagues too numerous to list who over the past forty years have contributed insights to my understanding of the menorah.

I pray that this book will enrich your life as you claim for yourself the Jewish heritage that was biblically described as the wealth of the nations.

Fraternally in the Messiah,
John D. Garr, Ph.D., Th.D.
Hunukkah 2001

Chapter 1

God's Lamp

Because of the extreme attention to detail given to the design of the menorah, it is clear that it is more a symbolic form, a work of art, rather than a mere cultic apparatus.[1] Moses was instructed by God to "make a lampstand of pure gold. The lampstand and its base and its shaft are to be made of hammered work . . . six branches shall go out from its sides; three branches of the lampstand from its one side, and three branches of the lampstand from its other side."[2]

The menorah is a concrete symbol of God himself, the source of light.[3] Its central lamp is called by the Jews *ner Elohim* (the lamp of God). David exclaimed, "You are my lamp, O Lord; the Lord turns my darkness into light,"[4] thereby identifying God with the menorah as he who illuminates the darkness. The Psalmist observed that God "wraps himself in light as with a garment."[5] Rather than bedeck himself in the brilliant colors associated with the pagan deities of the ancient world, God clothed himself in pure white light as a mantle.[6] God's divine presence, the *Shekhinah*, was manifest as a "fiery light."[7] When Ezekiel saw the temple, the earth shone with God's glory,[8] the same glory that the prophet saw as "fire."[9] God's majesty illuminated the temple as the fiery light of a golden lamp. The sages noted that the "Holy one, blessed be he, was constrained to dwell with mortals in the light of a lamp . . . and so a 'pure menorah' came down from heaven."[10]

Daniel declared of the Lord: "He reveals deep and hidden things . . . light dwells in him."[11] It is no coincidence that when this prophet viewed "the Ancient of Days," he observed that "his eyes were like flaming torches."[12] When John saw the throne of God and the Lamb, the apostle observed one with "seven eyes" that he identified as "a flame of fire,"[13] the "seven spirits of God."[14] Zechariah declared that these seven flames of fire are the "eyes of the Lord, which run to and fro through the earth."[15]

God's light and life, the essence of the divine nature, are graphically displayed in the menorah. One of the most significant and repeated metaphors used to describe God in Scripture is light. John declares it simply and directly: "God is light."[16] The pristine purity of white, transparent light is the most graphic material representation for the ultimately incomprehensible Deity. Not only do the Hebrew Scriptures continually describe God as being light, they also refer to the Messiah with metaphors of light, calling him a "star"[17] and the "sun of righteousness."[18]

Another perhaps even more significant metaphor for God is fire. He was a fiery voice in the burning bush.[19] He was a pillar of fire that was light to Israel and darkness to the Egyptian armies at the Reed Sea.[20] The smoke from his fire blackened the entire summit of Mount Sinai.[21] Both testaments assert that "our God is a consuming fire."[22] The Hebrew for "consuming fire," אֵשׁ אֹכֵל (*esh akal*), implies a magnificent conflagration–a bonfire as it were–that draws everything around it into its flames and releases enormous amounts of energy skyward. In like manner, God is *esh akal*, the fire that draws those who approach him into the all-consuming energy stream of the Holy Spirit, where they are filled with the fire of his presence and extend the praises heavenward.[23] The wonder of this experience, however, is that the all-consuming Fire never consumes those who are drawn into his presence. Like the burning bush in which he dwelt, he lives in them inflaming them with passion and vision so that from them radiate the fiery tongues of his divine Word.

The ancients recognized fire as one of their most important material assets because it could be maintained and exploited for personal conveniences, including light, warmth, cooking, and various crafts and trades. They also found fire to be one of the central elements of theophany.[24] When Daniel saw the throne of glory, it looked like a fiery flame, with wheels all ablaze.[25] Because fire brings both light and warmth, it reveals a God of love who enlightens the universe and warms those who come out of the darkness of the world into his loving embrace of light.

The menorah's seven flames are repeatedly used in the panorama of Holy Scripture to depict God himself. Explicit biblical identification of fiery lights symbolize God's glory. Though Israel's wilderness sanctuary was the first human shrine that did not focus on the image of a pagan deity, it, nevertheless, featured a symbol, an icon that pointed beyond itself to the invisible God. The menorah, the eternal light[26] can clearly be seen as a representation of the *Shekhinah*, God's indwelling presence among mankind.

WHOSE LAMP IS IT?

Because the menorah has been so closely identified as a Jewish symbol–and, indeed, has come to symbolize the nation of Israel itself–it has often been called the "Jewish" menorah. Believing it to be a symbol of an antiquated religion, most Christian teachers have seen little significance in the menorah for the church and have cast it with nonchalance into obscurity. By the same token, Jewish leaders have often been offended by occasional Christian use of the menorah, seeing such as a co-opting of sacred symbols and elements that were clearly given to the Jews by

God himself. Some even consider Christian use of menorahs as an expropriation of *sacramenta*, especially when they are used for purposes outside traditional Jewish understanding. But, is the name *Jewish menorah* wholly accurate?

The truth is that the menorah is God's lamp, as Scripture clearly declares: "The lamp of God . . . in the temple of the Lord, where the ark of God was . . ."[27] The menorah is not merely the Jewish candlestick or the tabernacle lampstand or the temple candelabrum. It is "God's lamp." It belongs to all of God's people, both Jews and Christians. Its rich symbolism is appropriate to both faith communities, representing God's light radiating into man's world, the power of vision and insight that comes to believers in God, both Jew and Gentile, through God's Word.

Assuring as the light of a torch along an unfamiliar trail on a moonless night, so does the Word of God give vision and direction to humankind, illuminating the narrow way that leads to the gates of eternal life.[28] Without clear insight into the Word of God, people perish.[29] When illumination from God's Word is not manifest, people lack prophetic vision, and when vision is not present, people stumble down the slippery slope of deception and plunge, often irrecoverably, off the precipice of misunderstanding. Because the Word of God is not of primary value to them, masses of humanity wantonly and recklessly throw themselves into the vortex of unrestrained passion. As a result, mankind reaps the natural consequences of a lack of vision or devotion to the things of God. On the other hand, happy are they who keep God's commandments,[30] allowing God's lamp to light their way and lead them on to eternal life.

The Word of God is like a light that shines in a dark place, clearly pointing the way. It channels the path of the just toward the "day star" who arises in the hearts of believers.[31] It dispels the darkness, the confusion, the ignorance, the fear, the superstition, and the dangers inherent in human existence. In spite of the ominous obscurity of the human situation, one small ray from the Eternal Word dispels the darkness, brings clarity of purpose, and unmistakably marks the way to the tree of life so clearly that no one who walks in that light will stumble.[32]

The menorah comes to symbolize the very salvation of God itself, for we are told by the prophet that God will not rest until the salvation of his people is manifest as a brightly burning lamp.[33] Since God was referring to salvation and to his own lamp, could it have been anything other than the menorah? The menorah–as well as the One whom it represents–offers a clear vision of God's salvation. Indeed, it is wisdom and knowledge in God's Word that brings stability and strengthens salvation.[34] Without the stabilizing element of God's Word, the believer is left vulnerable to the deceptive devices of "powers and principalities" and to the ever-changing winds of human surmising.[35] With the Word of God's vision, the believer is well-grounded upon a secure and stable foundation. Jesus declared that when one hears and does the Word of God ("my sayings"), he wisely constructs his life on the bedrock of divine revelation and insight that will stand against every tumultuous circumstance that life may bring.[36]

It is the Word of God that causes the path of the just to be evermore illuminated until the day of completeness.[37] The Word, as the menorah, continues to dispel the darkness along the believer's pathway until it brings him to the light of full day in the radiance of God's glory in the face of Jesus, the Anointed. One cannot be overcome by the prince of darkness when he follows the illumination of God's lamp.

When Jews and Christians see the menorah, they are assured that God's ordained lamp will direct their paths.[38] God will continue to provide the light of life for his people: "The Lord will be your everlasting light, and your God will be your glory."[39] God's Lamp will forever be man's light.

[1] Carol L. Meyers, *The Tabernacle Menorah* (Missoula, Montana: Scholars Press, 1976), p. 168.

[2] Exodus 25:31-32, New American Standard Version.

[3] Edwin R. Goodenough, *Jewish Symbols in the Greco-Roman Period* (New York: Pantheon Books, 1956), IV, p. 96. See also Lee I. Levine, *The Ancient Synagogue* (New Haven: Yale University Press, 2000), p. 572.

[4] 2 Samuel 22:29, New International Version.

[5] Psalm 104:2, New International Version.

[6] Thorlief Boman, *Hebrew Thought Compared with Greek* (Philadelphia: The Westminster Press, 1960), p. 89.

[7] Psalm 78:14. The New Revised Standard Version correctly translates the hendiadys אֵשׁ אוֹר (*'owr 'esh*) as "fiery light."

[8] Ezekiel 43:2.

[9] Ezekiel 1:27-28; 8:2-4.

[10] Goodenough, IV, p.89.

[11] Daniel 2:22, New International Version.

[12] Daniel 10:6, NAS.

[13] Revelation 1:14; 2:18, KJV

[14] Revelation 5:6.

[15] Zechariah 4:10, KJV.

[16] 1 John 1:5.

[17] Numbers 24:17.

[18] Malachi 4:2.

[19] Exodus 3:2-4.

[20] Exodus 13:21-22.

[21] Exodus 19:18.

[22] Deuteronomy 4:24; Hebrews 12:29.

[23] The basis of this analysis of "consuming fire" was shared with me by Dr. Charles Bryant-Abraham.

[24] Edwin R. Goodenough, IV, p. 91.

[25] Daniel 7:9.

[26] Carol L. Meyers, *The Tabernacle Menorah* (Missoula, Montana: Scholars Press, 1976), p. 177.

[27] 1 Samuel 3:1-3, KJV.

[28] Matthew 7:14.

[29] Proverbs 29:18.

[30] Proverbs 29:18.

[31] 2 Peter 1:19, KJV.

[32] Isaiah 35:8.

[33] Isaiah 62:1.

[34] Isaiah 33:6.

[35] Ephesians 4:14.

[36] Luke 6:48.

[37] Proverbs 4:18.

[38] Isaiah 60:19.

Chapter 2

Man's Light

The menorah is God's lamp and man's light because it is unique to God's character to give illumination, and it is essential to man's being that he have light. God is light, and in him is no darkness at all.[1] "The unfolding of [God's] words gives light; it imparts understanding to the simple."[2] The vision that God gives is so enlightening that "whoever walks the road, although a fool, shall not go astray."[3] When believers walk in the light, as God is in the light, they have fellowship with one another, and their sins are forgiven.[4] God's light removes the darkness of sin, and it produces unity among those who accept his illumination.

God's eternal will and plan for man has always been one of covenant and blessing, in which God's light illuminates man's life so that he may fully realize his destiny and continue in a face-to-face relationship with the Eternal Father. In the beginning, Adam and Eve were able to commune with God, basking in the light of his presence. He was their God and their light, much more than mere illumination: he was their peace, tranquility, repose, and joy. The primal light that existed before and outside of all creation, that unapproachable light of the Divine Glory, accompanied them in a covenantal relationship of complete blessing. God himself caused his countenance to shine upon them and gave them peace.

God's first material creation was the very substance of life. Without light, no life–plant or animal–could exist. Light is the sole source of energy that is essential for photosynthesis, the process that allows the planet's flora to flourish. Without photosynthesis in plants, no fauna would have food to fuel its existence. Light, then, was and is the very essence of life. Parallel with this primeval manifestation of life-giving physical light was the radiance of spiritual light that provided life and insight to Edenic man. Adam and Eve were intended to walk with God in the light of his presence.

Sin, however, invaded the sanctity of that relationship and sundered the divine connection. "Your sins have separated you from me,"[5] God declared. Since God could not look upon iniquity, Adam and Eve could no longer maintain a face-to-face relationship with their creator. They withdrew from God, leaving themselves woefully and abysmally alone in the void of the sin's darkness. The path to the tree of life, which the menorah later came to represent, was closed, and angelic sentries were posted to ensure the inaccessibility of its fruit.

When one stumbles in spiritual darkness, that darkness is gross, an all-pervasive sense of doom and gloom. Like a spelunker whose emergency light has been extinguished, the sinner is in a darkness that is tangible, and he is engrossed in abject hopelessness. Desperation gives way to the terror of darkness. When one chooses to live in spiritual darkness, it is not long before all vision fails, just as total blindness ensues when humans and other creatures are subjected to total physical darkness for any extended period of time. The ocular mechanisms atrophy and cannot be renewed. Likewise those who revel in spiritual darkness soon find themselves degenerate reprobates, incapable of vision.

Through the fall of Adam, all men were brought under the power of spiritual darkness.[6] The longing outcry of every human heart since that time has been for divine illumination, a flash of insight, a spark of communication with the Creator. Every human heart in history has exclaimed the anguished cry of King Balak to the prophet Balaam: "What has the Lord said?"[7] When God's face is hidden, when God's lamp is obscured, great is the darkness of the human heart, and void is human reason. The soul that is so darkened is capable of actions so vile that they defy description.

But, there is good news. God has ordained a lamp to illuminate his anointed ones.[8] God has chosen to draw near to himself his beloved creation who had withdrawn because of sin. Once again God permits small rays of his light to shine into human hearts. Initially this action came to men and women who sought God through repentance and prayer, causing the infallible word of prophecy, the light that shines in a dark place, to be manifest in their hearts as they were carried along by the Holy Spirit.[9] Throughout the course of history, God's Word has been a lamp to the feet of the righteous, lighting their pathway.[10]

There were many patriarchs and matriarchs of faith who encountered the Divine Light. Abel was given insight by the Divine to offer an acceptable sacrifice.[11] Enoch walked in God's light for 365 years before he was translated so as not to see death.[12] Noah found grace in God's eyes because he alone had remained pure in an evil world.[13] Job walked with God and found the light of divine insight before, during, and after his fiery trial.

God entered into an intimate relationship with man when Abraham, a Babylonian by birth and a Syrian by nationality, was called by the Divine Light to leave his country and go forth in search of a land of promise and a city whose foundations had been laid by God himself.[14] On the day in which the Abrahamic covenant was established, God himself, in the form of a blazing torch (the *Shekhinah*), walked between the pieces of Abraham's sacrifice, flooding the patriarch of faith with the light of his presence.[15] Perhaps that torch was a spiritual/material foreshadowing of the menorah.

In time, God determined to disclose his illuminating instructions for mankind that outlined the conditions on which he might be approached by man. First, he appeared to Moses and spoke to him in the tongues[16] of fire that issued forth from the burning bush. The sevenfold Spirit of God spoke fiery words of light, bringing the hope of deliverance and liberty to Abraham's descendants. Those golden words must have seemed like a shining menorah both to Moses and to his fellow Israelites.

It is always from the fire that God speaks; therefore, it is imperative that one learns to listen to the fire in order to hear God's voice. The voice that issued forth the divine commission of Moses, however, merely reiterated and fortified the fire that had been burning in the once proud prince of Egypt since early childhood. Though he had been afforded a lofty position of privilege, wealth, erudition, and power as Pharaoh's grandson, Moses chose instead the "reproach of Christ,"[17] identifying with the pain and sufferings of his own people. God had orchestrated the positioning of the infant in Pharaoh's house and had arranged that his nurse should be his own mother, so that he would be taught his own heritage. One day, the fire that burned in his bosom erupted in flaming rage and violence against an Egyptian taskmaster, and Moses was forced to flee Egypt. After forty years of preparation as a shepherd in the Sinai desert, the prophet was ready to listen to the fire that had long been his own passion as it communicated the divine strategy that would effect Israel's deliverance. The fiery words from the burning bush resounded to Israel and have echoed down the corridors of time to all peoples enslaved in oppression's darkness. The immortal liberating light burst forth in fiery words: "Let my people go!"

Later at Sinai, with the descendants of Abraham assembled before him, God thundered ten words of instruction in tongues of fire which were also written "with the finger of God" upon tablets of stone.[18] According to tradition the Ten Commandments resounded in seventy languages to the world's nations, the children of the seventy descendants of Noah's sons.[19] These words were both heard and seen by the Israelites. Literally, the Hebrew text that records this synesthetic incident translates: "And the people saw the voices [*kol*] and the flames."[20] How does one see voices? Philo of Alexandria, before the time of Christ, said, "From the fire . . . there sounded a voice, for the flame became articulate speech . . . so clearly were the words formed . . . that they seemed to see them rather than hear them."[21] Perhaps recounting the Sinai incident, Jeremiah observed, "Is not [God's] word like fire . . . and like a hammer which shatters a rock?"[22] God's Word took the physical appearance of tongues of fire and codified one of history's greatest documents, the Ten Commandments. With the Decalogue, men were equipped with understanding of how to love God and how to love man, thereby fulfilling both the two greatest commandments[23] and the one overarching divine instruction: "Love."[24]

The light of the menorah corresponded to the Torah. In one rabbinic midrash, God said to Moses: "Say to thy brother Aaron: Greater than the gifts of the princes is thy gift; for thou art called upon to kindle the light, and, while the sacrifices shall last only as long as the Temple lasts, thy light of the Law shall last forever."[25] The Torah light is the eternal flame that ever illuminates men's pathway.

The Ten Commandments were designed to make the abhorrence of sin abundantly clear[26] and to elicit repentance from men who with a whole heart would seek God. The entirety of God's instruction (Torah) became man's spiritual light. Solomon summarized God's grace in giving his ten instructions to men: "For the commandment is a lamp and the teaching a light, and the reproofs of discipline are the way of life."[27] God's commandments are clear, "enlightening the eyes."[28] The fiery Sinai words, then, were a menorah in themselves, illuminating both the nation of Israel and the entire world. Even those nations that would not accept God's Torah as Israel did heard the fundamental words of thunder in their own languages and had those precepts emblazoned on their hearts so that since that time, their consciences have either condemned or exonerated them.[29]

Finally, in the fullness of time, God made the complete disclosure of his very essence and glory when he spoke to all mankind through his only begotten Son, Jesus Messiah of Israel and the Savior of the world. The glory of God was fully revealed in Jesus.[30] "He who has seen me, has seen the Father,"[31] Jesus declared. Is it any wonder, then, that Jesus declared himself to be "the light of the world"? The first incarnation of God's Word, the eternal Torah that had been with the Father before creation and had subsequently been revealed to prophets and wise men of Israel, became incarnate in the person of *Yeshua HaMashiach* (Jesus the Christ).

When gross spiritual darkness covered the earth, the glory of the Lord arose over Israel in the person of Jesus who uniquely became a personal light, "the light of life,"[32] to all who believed in him. The sin that had separated men from the presence of God was removed through Jesus' atoning death, making it possible for God to impute the righteousness of Jesus to them.[33] At the moment that faith is released, the darkness covering the human heart is dispelled with the same power and finality as the darkness that covered the face of the deep dissipated when God commanded, "Let there be light." The face-to-face relationship with the Divine that was lost in the first Adam is restored in the new Adam, Jesus the Messiah.[34] The light that had withdrawn, leaving only abject darkness, suddenly reappears, bringing a flash of illumination that overpowers the human heart and emotion with "unspeakable joy, full of glory."[35]

From God's Lamp radiates God's Light that becomes man's light. As David declared, "For with thee is the fountain of life: in thy light shall we see light."[36] The fountain of life that sprang from the presence of the Eternal Father in the person of the only begotten Son fully manifested the light of God's presence so that men were–and continue to be–enlightened. God's Lamp, the incarnate menorah, brought the essence of heaven down to earth. He became man's light so that men from every tribe and tongue have been illuminated and brought into the Divine Presence with the promise of being clothed with the same glory of eternal light and life that Adam once had that is fully manifest in Jesus, God's Lamp and man's light.

[1] 1 John 1:5.
[2] Psalm 119:130, New Revised Standard Version.
[3] Isaiah 35:8, New King James Version.
[4] 1 John 1:7.
[5] Isaiah 59:2.
[6] Romans 5:12.
[7] Numbers 23:17, New Revised Standard Version.
[8] Psalm 132:17.
[9] 2 Peter 1:19.
[10] Psalm 119:105.
[11] Genesis 4:4.
[12] Genesis 5:24.
[13] Genesis 6:8-9.
[14] Hebrews 11:8-10.
[15] Genesis 15:17.
[16] Exodus 3:2-4.
[17] Hebrews 11:26.
[18] Exodus 31:18.
[19] Genesis 10.

[20] Exodus 20:18, literal translation.

[21] Philo, The Decalogue, F. Colson, trans., *Philo* (Cambridge, Harvard University Press, 1968) vol. 7, pp. 28-29.

[22] Jeremiah 23:29, New American Standard.

[23] Matthew 22:36-40.

[24] Romans 13:10; 1 Chronicles 13:13.

[25] *Tanhuma* (ed. Martin Buber), in *Jewish Encyclopedia: A Descriptive Record of the History, Religion, Literature, and Customs of the Jewish People from the Earliest Times to the Present Day*, ed. Isidore Singer, New York, 1901), I, p. 4.

[26] Romans 7:13.

[27] Proverbs 6:23, New Revised Standard.

[28] Psalm 19:8.

[29] Romans 2:14-15.

[30] 2 Corinthians 4:6.

[31] John 14:9.

[32] John 8:12.

[33] Romans 4:11.

[34] 1 Corinthians 15:22-45.

[35] 1 Peter 1:8.

[36] Psalm 36:9, KJV.

Chapter 3
Divine Design

The menorah has the distinction of being the only emblem in either Jewish or Christian worship and tradition that
was designed by God himself. All other emblems represent
man's response to God's call, symbols that memorialize great
events of history or that serve as material objects designed to
fulfill divine imperatives. In Judaism, the *mezuzah* fulfills in
literal terms the commandment to write the law on the door-
posts of one's house[1] and is a daily reminder to the Jewish
people of God's constant protection of their homes. In Christianity, the cross serves as a reminder of the atoning death of
Jesus and of the believer's dependence upon that one work of
redemption as the sole foundation for his faith.

The menorah, however, had a heavenly manifestation
that long predated its first earthly display. It likely first appeared when God's Word created the heavens and the earth
and instituted the form of worship that the heavenly hosts
have always extended to the Creator. Eternally prominent
in this heavenly display were seven flames of resplendent
glory pointing beyond themselves to the enthroned Deity.[2]

THE BLUEPRINT FROM HEAVEN

The term *candlestick* used in most English transla-
tions is an anachronism as well as a misnomer, for the meno-

rah was not a candle holder, but a lampstand, featuring oil lamps with wicks in the ancient tradition of illumination. The original menorah probably had bowls of oil atop its branches with a floating wick in each bowl. Later versions likely featured a channel through which the oil in the bowls was drawn to the wick. This would have allowed for the positioning of the lights in different directions.

God gave specific instructions to Moses, vividly detailing the design for the menorah.[3] Considering the amount of text that is given to a description of its design and its substance, this appliance was apparently of paramount importance to the sanctuary. When the comprehensive blueprint was completed, the prophet was commanded: "See that you make them according to the pattern shown you on the mountain."[4] This phrase was spoken of the menorah alone among all the sanctuary appliances. Not even the ark of the covenant or the cherubim of the most holy place required such precise duplication. Then, only chapters later, the vivid description was repeated as if to underscore by emphasis the menorah's importance.[5]

We are left to infer from Moses' account of his experience that he was invited to peer into the heavens where he saw the divine archetype for praise, worship, and service, the system employed by the angels from the beginning of time. The Apostolic Writings speak of this event: "Moses, when he was about to erect the tent, was warned, 'See that you make everything according to the pattern that was shown you on the mountain.' "[6] Of all the many splendors of heaven that Moses was allowed to view and to replicate, it is certainly significant that the injunction to "make all things according to the pattern" immediately followed only the command to build the menorah.

The heavenly throne was, no doubt, the source of Moses' inspiration, the pattern according to which he was to build everything in the tent of meeting, especially the menorah. The altar of incense was also patterned after the "golden altar" in heaven on which, according to John, angels offer the prayers of the saints.[7] The ark of the covenant with its mercy seat and two covering cherubim was patterned after the throne of the Almighty. The menorah design, then, must have had a significant role in the divine worship which Moses observed when he was transported in spirit into the heavenly realm.

Centuries later, John, the disciple whom Jesus loved, had a similar experience on the Isle of Patmos, a moving account of which is chronicled in the Apocalypse. First, the apostle was overwhelmed by a spectacular manifestation of the resurrected Messiah, whom he observed standing in the midst of seven golden lampstands.[8] Then John, like Moses, was invited to "come up" and to view heaven itself, where he saw seven spectacular flames of fire burning before God's throne. John was told that these seven eternally blazing lamps are the "seven spirits of God"[9] that are "sent forth into all the earth."[10]

Isaiah enumerated the seven spirits of God as (1) the Spirit of the Lord, (2) the spirit of wisdom, (3) the spirit of understanding, (4) the spirit of counsel, (5) the spirit of strength, (6) the spirit of knowledge, and (7) the spirit of the fear of God.[11] If the Spirit of the Lord is considered to be in the middle lamp, the shaft of the menorah, there are three spirits on one side of the shaft and three on the other. Given in the order of Isaiah's listing, the three spirits on one side (wisdom, counsel, and understanding) speak of concept while the three spirits on the other side (knowledge, strength, fear of God) deal with practice.[12]

Could it be that the "seven" spirits are sent forth into "all the earth" to replicate the heavenly will on earth by introducing the light of divine revelation to illuminate the human soul? The prayer Jesus taught his disciples declares that God's will is to be performed on earth in a manner parallel with that manifest in heaven.[13] The menorah that Moses constructed on earth replicated the prototype in heaven. Likewise, the seven spirits before the throne of God proceed into all the earth, bringing his divine light to all mankind.

Interestingly, then, both Moses and John recounted similar descriptions of heaven, despite the fact that their experiences were separated by some 1600 years. In both cases, the first and perhaps most prominent thing they described were the seven lamps of fire, the pattern for the menorah. If this pattern had such profound significance in heaven that its replication on earth was to be precisely according to the pattern revealed in heaven, a small leap of logic would suggest that this instrument should also play a significant role for those on earth who seek to worship the Creator.

DESIGN DETAILS

The menorah was a masterpiece of beauty and craftsmanship. In studying the physical details of the menorah's design, however, it is important to give priority to the thoroughly Hebraic idea that its function was more important than its form. While classical Greek thought focused on physical appearance and gave great and picturesque detailed descriptions, the Hebraic approach to material reality was to focus on function rather than form. This is true of the menorah in all of its design details. Even the word *menorah* is verbal rather than nominal based. Virtually all Hebrew words can usually be traced to a three-letter verbal root. The word מְנוֹרָה (*menorah*) is actually a phrase using the common verbal stem ניר or נור (*nyr* or *nur*, modern *ner*) to which is added the *mem*-preformative (מ). The literal meaning of *nyr* is "to flame." The term is closely connected with the idea of a torch, a material object which supports and casts a flame that produces light. With the addition of the letter *mem*, the word is menorah, meaning essentially a repository or support for the flaming (lamp).

Though the menorah design was given and repeated

in much detail,[14] the descriptions are fairly ambiguous, making it difficult to imagine exactly how it looked.[15] Midrashic accounts even suggest that Moses himself found it difficult to follow God's instructions until he was shown the heavenly menorah of fire as a prototype of what he was to construct.[16] This lack of detailed graphic description accounts for the diverse depictions of the menorah both in history and at the present time.

At any rate, the first sanctuary menorah was constructed by Bezalel, the master craftsman, who was guided by the wisdom of God that is said to have paralleled that with which God himself created the universe. "I have filled [Bezalel] with the Spirit of God in wisdom, in understanding, in knowledge, and in all kinds of craftsmanship,"[17] God said. The name *Bezalel* has been interpreted to mean "in the shadow of God" and indicated that the artisan had the ability to make the menorah because he had a special relation or access to the divine light.[18] Bezalel's insights must have been divinely inspired, for the lampstand that he constructed is generally viewed as impossible to replicate.

The menorah that served as the only light in the tabernacle was to be hammered (*miksheh*) of one solid piece of "pure gold" (*zahav tahor*).[19] No other appurtenance of the sanctuary was described in this way. The use of *tahor* may not have referred to gold in a purely metallurgical sense, however. It could be related to "brightness" in a visual, and perhaps even cosmic, sense.[20]

The menorah was to have seven lamps of fire atop seven branches, six of which foliated from the one central stem, which itself was called the lampstand. The branches were to be richly embellished with chalices in the form of almond blossoms[21] and other decorations, including capitals (knobs) that were almost certainly shaped like apples. The flowers decorating the uppermost cups on the branches were also to serve as receptacles for the seven lamps.

The structural members of the menorah are indicated in Hebrew by the word קָנֶה (*kaneh*), which is the likely source of the English word *cane*. קָנֶה is Hebrew for "reed," and refers to the Persian reed, common to the Sinai Peninsula,[22] which had multiple uses in the ancient world, serving as staff, spear, measuring device,[23] a beam for weight scales,[24] and other devices.

The Masoretic Hebrew text indicates that the shaft is the menorah, from which six branches foliate. This is further confirmed by the use of the term יָרֵךְ (*yarekh*) in the description of the menorah: ". . .the menorah . . . his shaft [*yerekhakh*], and his branches [*kanim*]."[25]

The almond-flower chalices on the branches and atop the menorah were called גְּבִיעִם (*gebi'im,* singular *gabea*) in Hebrew. It is likely a word of Egyptian derivation, meaning a "libation vessel"[26] and should be rendered "chalice," "goblet," or "bowl," not "cup" (the Hebrew for which is כּוֹס *kos*). This is the term which describes the silver vessel which Joseph directed his servants to place in his brother Benjamin's sack.[27] Rabbinic tradition suggests that the cups were like "Alexandrian goblets."[28]

Another decorative device for the menorah was the כַּפְתֹּרִם (*kaphtorim*), "capitals (as at the top of a column) or knobs." These decorations, connected with the chalices, were also said to be "apple-shaped." Rabbinic tradition says that these capitals resembled "Cretan apples" or "eggs."[29] It has been suggested that these capitals were originally fashioned after the calyxes that hold the flowers of the moriah plant, which have the appearance of knobs.[30] On each of the six branches were three round capitals that were associated with chalices shaped like almond flowers. The arrangement is replicated four times in the central shaft and is repeated three times in each of the six foliating branches.

Whether this description indicates three round (apple-shaped) chalices with the appearance of almond flowers or three round apple-shaped capitals in addition to three chalices in addition to three flowers is not clear. If the former is preferred, there are three decorations on each branch, and the total on the menorah would then correspond to the rabbinic assertion of 42.[31] If the latter is correct, the total decorative devices would correspond to Josephus' seventy.[32] This figure is obtained by adding the three sets of cups, flowers, and capitals on each of the six branches (54 ornaments) to four similar sets on the shaft, making 69. The seventieth ornament was likely a special embellishment around the lamp's shaft,[33] possibly identical with the golden "seventh socket" mentioned in the Septuagint.[34]

Based on the carved reliefs on the Arch of Titus, it has been asserted that the menorah rested on a two-tiered hexagonal base. This rendition is considered to be accurate because the "double-step motif as a candlestick podium rarely if ever appears in Roman statuary."[35] On the other hand, there is both archaeological evidence and rabbinic commentary to suggest that the base may have been triangular, shaped more like a tripod. Some tradition suggests that the menorah had an indeterminate number of feet extending from its base, which would serve to support the tripod base theory.[36] Others maintain that the menorah stood on three feet, shaped like lions' paws.[37] Rashi declared that the Hebrew word for the menorah's base, *yerekh*, means a plate with three legs.[38] Additionally, archaeological discoveries in Jerusalem have confirmed that earlier menorahs were tripodal.[39] Others have suggested that both the tripod base and the two-tiered hexagonal base may be correct, with the hexagonal base added to the original tripod to give it additional stability.

The seven lamps added to the menorah gave it even deeper significance. The lamps were symbolic, proclaiming a message of light to all men, Jew and Gentile.[40] Jewish sages suggest that the seven lamps demonstrate a power parallel with the seven creative words that begin the Bible,[41] as well as the six days of creation plus *Shabbat*.

The Arch of Titus' portrayal of the menorah and other artifacts brought to Rome after the Roman general destroyed the temple in 70 C.E.

According to rabbinic tradition, the menorah had the following dimensions: its height was 18 handbreadths or 3 cubits (4.5 feet). Its width (the spread of its outermost branches) was 2 cubits (3 feet).[42] The branches were approximately 3 inches thick. The menorah that was in the temple in the time of Jesus weighed 1 talent (76 pounds).[43]

MENORAH DEPICTIONS

The actual physical appearance of the menorah has been the object of much speculation. Traditionally, it has been viewed as having three curved semicircular branches on both sides of a central shaft or lampstand. Some have suggested that the central shaft rose to higher than the six attached branches. The majority of opinions, however, has held that each branch rose to the same level as the central shaft so that all seven lamps burned in a straight line.[44]

This opinion is reinforced by the bas-relief on Titus' Arch of Triumph (*porta triumphalis*) that was erected around 81 C.E. on the Forum in Rome at death and apotheosis of the Roman conquerer who destroyed Jerusalem and the temple in 70 C.E.[45] This arch depicts the seven-branched menorah among the various spoils from the temple which Titus brought to Rome following his triumph over the Jewish insurrection. Generally, Roman triumphal arches were designed to be historical documents; therefore, artisans endeavored to make accurate depictions. The details of the Titus Arch indicate the sculptors' intimate knowledge of the temple vessels as they are described in the Bible and other Jewish sources.[46]

It is suggested that the depiction of the base is inaccurate; however, arguments have been advanced on the other side of the debate. Since the oversized base is in such blatant conflict with classical aesthetics, it is thought to be inconceivable that Roman craftsmen would have invented them. Another argument against the Titus design is the presence of various animal figures in the panels of the base. Would Torah prohibitions against images have been circumvented in the construction of the temple menorah? The Mishnaic tractate *Abodah Zarak* (idolatry) permits concave and forbids convex images: if they protrude, they are "graven images," while if they are hollowed out, they are not. The images included on the menorah base panels in the Titus Arch are within those parameters. It is very likely that Herod the Great's positive disposition toward things Roman led him to introduce symbols of Roman authority and values on the temple menorah.[47]

This theory of the design, however, has been challenged by those who believe that the actual temple menorah was hidden before the fall of Jerusalem, just as the original menorah in the first temple was said to have been hidden by Jeremiah before Nebuchadnezzar's invasion. This view holds that what Titus carried to Rome was a substitute with an altered design. Whatever the case may be, it is interesting that following the destruction of the second temple, the menorah (not the star of David, as so many erroneously believe) became the "principal decorative art symbol of the Jewish faith."[48] It is also ironic that this design of the

The Arch of Titus erected on the Forum in Rome around 81 C.E.

menorah memorialized as part of Titus' booty from a conquered Israel is today employed on the official seal of the restored State of Israel, a symbol of the "undying and irresistible force of light."[49]

The semicircular design for the branches of the menorah is reinforced by many archaeological discoveries dating to pre-Christian times. It has been found on coins struck in pre-Christian times, in Jewish catacombs of Rome, and in the third-century Palestinian synagogue at Dura Europos.[50] Indeed, the most ancient depiction of the menorah extant is that on the Hasmonean coins struck by Antigonus. These coins feature a menorah with semicircular branches but with a tripod base. Perhaps this is the basis of the sages' insistence that the menorah rested on thee legs.[51]

Various Jewish sages, most notably Maimonides,[52] the twelfth century Talmudist and philosopher, have suggested, however, that the menorah's appearance was totally different from what is commonly believed. They insist that it was comprised of a central shaft from both sides of which three straight branches emerged at acute angles to the shaft to reach the same height as the central lampstand. In his commentary on the Torah,[53] Rashi, the eleventh century

Menorah design portrayed on the Titus Arch in Rome.

Jewish commentator, explicitly declared that the branches "extended upward in a diagonal." The fact that the Hebrew word translated "branches" (*kanim*) can be interpreted as "a straight line" is enlisted as support for this theory. In his commentary to *Terumah*, Rabbi Avraham ben Mosheh ben Maimon, Maimonides' son, insisted that "the six branches . . . extended upward from the center shaft of the menorah in a straight line, as depicted by my father, and not in a semicircle as depicted by others."[54]

Menorah design as viewed by Maimonides and other Jewish scholars.

Whatever the case may have been, there is no doubt that a lampstand featuring seven branches with seven lamps was the only light of the wilderness sanctuary. It is also undeniable that the original tabernacle lampstand replicated the supernal menorah and that it was designed by God himself. The menorah was and remains God's idea. Interestingly, the menorah is the only sacred symbol that has never been polluted or used for occult purposes.

Despite its significance in the tabernacle and the two temples, the menorah is now more motif than apparatus in the minds of the Jewish people. It symbolizes God's eternal vigilance to bring light and life to his people. It also demonstrates Israel's dependence on the power of light to conquer evil. The menorah, then, is a powerful living emblem of divine design, God's lamp, man's light.

[1] Deuteronomy 11:20.
[2] Revelation 4:5.
[3] Exodus 25:31-40.
[4] Exodus 25:40, New International Version.
[5] Exodus 37:17-24.
[6] Hebrews 8:5, New Revised Standard Version.
[7] Revelation 5:8; 8:3, 4.
[8] Revelation 1:12, 13.
[9] Revelation 4:5.
[10] Revelation 5:6.
[11] Isaiah 11:2-3.
[12] S. R. Hirsch, *Collected Writings*, pp. 209-235, quoted at the Website: *http://members.tripod.com/~TheHOPE/menorah2.htm*, p. 4.
[13] Matthew 6:10.
[14] Exodus 25:31-40; 37:17-24.
[15] Daniel Sperber, "The History of the Menorah," *The Journal of Jewish Studies*, XVI, Nos. 3, 4, 1965, p. 135.

[16] Ginzberg, *Legends of the Jews* (1946). Quoted in Daniel Sperber, p. 135.

[17] Exodus 31:3.

[18] Erwin R. Goodenough, *Jewish Symbols in the Greco-Roman Period* (New York: Pantheon Books, 1954), Vol. IV, p. 91.

[19] Exodus 25:36.

[20] Carol L. Meyers, *The Tabernacle Menorah* (Missoula, Montana: Scholars Press, 1976), p. 168.

[21] See *www.shofar.org/shalom/8611_menorah.htm.* p.1.

[22] Carol L. Meyers, p. 19.

[23] Ezekiel 40-42.

[24] Isaiah 46:6.

[25] Exodus 25:31.

[26] Carol L. Meyers, p. 22. See endnote p. 35.

[27] Genesis 44:2, 16.

[28] Babylonian Talmud, *Menahoth* 28b.

[29] *Ibid.*

[30] Nogah Hareuveni, *The Emblem of the State of Israel: Its Roots in the Nature and Heritage of Israel* (Kiryat Ono, Israel: Keot Kedumim, 1988), 16-17.

[31] Rudolph Brasch, *The Judaic Heritage* (New York: David McKay Co., 1969), p. 315.

[32] L. Yarden, *The Tree of Light* (Ithaca, New York: Cornell University Press, 1971), p. 10.

[33] *Ibid.*

[34] Jeremiah 52:19, Septuagint Version.

[35] Daniel Sperber, p. 147.

[36] Babylonian Talmud, *Menachot* 28b. See also Internet Website: *www.acs.ucalgary.ca/~elsegal/Shokel/951215_Menorah.html* p 1.

[37] Henrich Strauss, *Encyclopaedia Judaica*, CDRom edition, section on "Menorah."

[38] *Ibid.*

[39] L. Yarden, p. 11.

[40] Rudolph Brasch, p. 311.

[41] *Ibid.*, p. 316.

[42] Bar. *Di-Meleketh ha -Mishkan* X, p. 64. Babylonian Talmud, 28b.

[43] L. Yarden, p. 10.

[44] S. R. Hirsch, p. 1.

[45] L. Yarden, p. 6.

[46] See the Internet Website: *www.acs.ucalgary.ca/~elsegal/Shokel/951215_Menorah.html*, p.1

[47] *Ibid.*

[48] See the Internet Website: *www.shofar.org/shalom/8611_menorah.htm* p. 2.

[49] Rudlolph Brasch, p. 309.

[50] *Ibid.*

[51] Maimonides, *Hilekhoth Beth Ha-Bechirah*, 3, 2.

[52] *Ibid.*

[53] *Terumah* 25:32.

[54] See the Web site: *www.his.com.*

Chapter 4

Pure Gold

While other implements in the sanctuary were to be overlaid with gold, only the menorah was to be made of one solid piece of pure gold: "All of [the menorah] was one beaten work of pure gold."[1] This quality of the menorah's construction is also rich with symbolic meaning for both Jews and Christians.

In three passages of Scripture, the menorah is called "the pure menorah."[2] That it was to be of pure gold demonstrates the fact that God demands purity wherever light is to be manifest. Among the Jewish people, purity of motive is considered essential to prayer and worship. This is manifest in the intensity and concentration on the Divine that is called *kavanah*. Lackadaisical attitudes and ambivalence are never conducive to enlightenment. Likewise, mere mindless repetition of words[3] and actions[4] leads only to meaningless confusion. When the Eternal is worshipped with a meek and contrite heart,[5] that worship is efficacious and elicits divine response. Peter encapsulated the Jewish idea of *kavanah* when he declared that the effectual, fervent prayer of a righteous person, a "contrite heart,"[6] is powerful.[7] Pure, intense worship and prayer always result in enlightenment and its accompanying blessing.

Focused, passionate devotion in worship helps one ful-

fill God's first and greatest commandment: "You shall love
the Lord your God."[8] Immediately before he gave this *mega-
mitzvah*, God spoke the immortal word that has echoed in
every Jewish heart since that time, "*Shema*." Literally *shema*
means "hear and obey." The one thing that God has always
wanted man to hear and obey is this word: "The Lord our God
is one Lord. You shall love the Lord your God with all your
heart, and with all your soul, and with all your strength."[9]

As an aid to concentration and *kavanah* in prayer, Jews
begin their most important prayer, the *Amidah*[10] by taking three
small steps backward and then three small steps forward to
remind themselves that they are entering the presence of the
King of the universe. Then while they are praying, they en-
gage in davening, swaying to and fro, mimicking the action of
candle's flame while moving every bone, muscle, and sinew
of their bodies. In this way, they demonstrate that they are
praying and worshipping with every fiber of their being, even
with a fiery fervency.

This intensity in worship was demonstrated materi-
ally in the refining fire that rendered the pure gold for the
pure menorah. In order to obtain "pure gold," ancient smelt-
ers subjected the precious metal to the refiner's fire exactly seven times. David revealed his knowledge of the
metallurgy of his day in the simile he used to describe the
purity of God's Word: "The words of the Lord are pure
words, like silver refined in an earthen furnace, purified
seven times."[11] The Word that enlightens is a Word purified by the seven flames of the sevenfold Spirit.

Zechariah also spoke of the smelting of silver and gold
as a metaphor for God's refining his people to a state of
absolute purity.[12] Only those who permit God to "turn up
the heat" so that impurities surface and are removed will
find themselves spiritually becoming the pure gold of which
the living menorah must be constructed. These are that part
of Israel and the church which the prophet predicted would

be forged and refined through the fire. It is only by the trials of God's Word and the strenuous testing of character that God allows to impact believers' lives that purity of heart is manifest and strengthened.

Abraham underwent such a testing in the *Akedah*, the binding of Isaac. It was through this process of testing that the Eternal proved the mettle of Abraham's heart, the quality that God knew was already there and needed only to be revealed. God did not need to test Abraham, for the Omniscient had already known Abraham before his conception. It was Abraham who needed to test Abraham; it was Abraham who needed to know Abraham. The request that he sacrifice his only son was the fire of Abraham's most severe trial; however, it revealed the purity of Abraham's heart not only for Abraham but also for all posterity. From this test and henceforth forever more, the heavenly Father came to be called "The God of Abraham."[13]

Often, however, from the testing fire that God brings into the lives of believers emerge ugly, despicable things. Again, this is only a part of the refining process in which the fire brings the dross to the surface so that it may be ladled off and cast away. When God exposes a weakness in one's life, it is designed not to destroy, but to purify. God is always refining his people, but his goal is to manifest their hearts before him as "pure gold." If one is pure in heart, as were Shadrach, Meshach, and Abednego, he can pass through a sevenfold flame of trial and still not smell of smoke.[14]

This is why the Jewish people have never approached God thinking to impress him with the splendor of their dress or their external appearance (as many Gentile cultures have historically done in worshipping their deities). The adornment of a meek and quiet spirit is far more impressive in the presence of God.[15] Jews wear a simple white prayer shawl, which they view as a "garment of light." There is no distinction of social status or political power that is manifest in more ostentatious dress.

Complete focus on the majesty and holiness of the Eternal is the aim of worship among the Jewish people. The idea in Judaism is to revere, not merely to understand God. The goal is to "know" God, not "know about God." Worship is not worship, therefore, without *kavanah's* pure, golden intensity, the focus within the human heart.

This truth was emphasized by Jesus: ". . . true worshipers shall worship the Father in spirit and in truth."[16] Literally translated, this passage declares that true worshipers worship in "spiritual truth."[17] This is parallel with John the Baptizer's prediction that Jesus would immerse his disciples in the fiery Holy Spirit. The Holy Spirit is fire, and the truth is spirit. When one is immersed in the Holy Spirit, he is immersed in fire. When one worships in spirit, he worships in truth as well.

The demand for *kavanah* in prayer and worship is also manifest in the Hebrew and Greek words for worship,[18] both of which mean to prostrate oneself in the presence of the King. It is the "pure in heart" who will "see God."[19] Every man who has the hope of salvation "purifies himself," even as God is pure.[20] Those who seek God with *kavanah* find that they are processed by the Holy Spirit in the refiner's fire that brings them forth as pure gold. This is the people whom God will "refine . . . as silver is refined" and whom he will "try . . . as gold is tried," so that when the process is complete, God will say of them, "It is my people."[21] It is to these people that God will reveal the light of his presence, the wisdom from above that is "first pure."[22]

In the ancient world, gold was the most precious of metals, prized by people of power and prestige. Accordingly, gold was used in ancient Israel to symbolize the high value placed by Israelite society on personal and communal worship of God Almighty. The golden candelabrum is symbolic of the priceless nature of the enlightenment God brings to those who fear him. Solomon's advice was to "buy the truth," along with wisdom, instruction, and understanding, and "sell it not."[23] Truth is precious and always comes at a price, sometimes the ultimate price.

The high value of purity and the weighty importance of this light in the world is exemplified in the requirement that the menorah be covered with a *tekhelet*[24] (blue) cloth when not in use. The dye that was used to achieve the biblical *tekhelet* was profoundly rare and expensive, usually reserved for royalty in the ancient world.[25] To obtain one gram of this dye, 8,500 *murex trunculus* sea mollusks[26] were painstakingly drilled to extract the minuscule secretion from their hypobranchial glands. The resulting "true blue" dye was worth up to twenty times its weight in gold.[27] By covering the menorah with a *tekhelet* cloth, God demonstrated the priceless nature of this light-bearing device.

David declared, "The ordinances of the Lord are true and righteous altogether. More to be desired are they than gold, even much fine gold."[28] He also exclaimed, "The law from your mouth is more precious to me than thousands of pieces of silver and gold."[29] Solomon described it thus: "How much better it is to get wisdom than gold!"[30]

According to tradition, the menorah could be constructed of metals other than gold in times of necessity; however, a menorah could never be fabricated from scrap metal.[31] This is a clear lesson for believers that God's light can never illuminate the world from the small remnants of time and energy that remain after they have been consumed with the cares of life and the pursuit of pleasures. Only that which is pure and costly, the very essence of life, is qualified to manifest the divine light.

Every microscopic particle of gold in the menorah has the potential for becoming the light of the world. When believers are connected to the Word of God–to Jesus, who is God's light–and when they permit the Holy Spirit to pu-

rify them and fill them with the oil of his gladness, they
will be lights in a world of darkness. The pure menorah
hammered from pure gold is God's lamp, man's light.

[1] Exodus 37:17.

[2] Exodus 31:8; 39:37; Leviticus 24:4.

[3] As in the chanting of a *mantra* in Eastern Monism.

[4] As in genuflections and exercises in self flagellation.

[5] Psalm 34:18; Isaiah 57:15.

[6] Psalm 51:17; Isaiah 57:15; 66:2.

[7] James 5:16.

[8] Deuteronomy 6:5; Mark 12:30.

[9] Deuteronomy 6:4-5.

[10] *Amidah* means standing; therefore, this is the one prayer which is always
said standing. The *Amidah* is also called the *Shemoneh Esreh* (Eighteen Bene-
dictions).

[11] Psalm 12:6, author's translation. See New International Version and New
American Standard Version.

[12] Zechariah 13:9.

[13] Hebrews 11:16.

[14] Daniel 3:27.

[15] 1 Peter 3:3-4.

[16] John 4:23.

[17] The phrase "spirit and truth" is the figure of speech *hendiadys*, in which one
of the terms modifies or is in apposition to the other; hence, "spiritual truth" or
"the spirit, the truth."

[18] The Hebrew for worship is שָׁחָה (*shachah*). The Greek for worship is
προσκυνέω (*proskuneo*).

[19] Matthew 5:8.

[20] 1 John 3:3.

[21] Zechariah 13:9.

[22] James 3:17.

[23] Proverbs 23:23.

[24] For a detailed account of the history and purpose of *tekhelet*, see the chapter,
"A Ribband of Blue" in my book, *The Hem of His Garment: Touching the
Power in God's Word* (Atlanta: Golden Key Books, 2000), pp. 45-51.

[25] Hence the name royal blue.

[26] Babylonian Talmud, *Sefer Moed*, Shabbat 85a.

[27] Baruch Sterman, "*Tekhelet*," on the Internet Website: *www.tekhelles.org.il*,
p. 2.

[28] Psalm 19:10, New Revised Standard Version.

[29] Psalm 119:72, New International Version.

[30] Proverbs 16:16.

[31] S. R. Hirsch, *Collected Writings*, pp. 209-235, quoted on the Internet
Website: *members.tripod.com/~The HOPE/menorah.htm*, p. 1.

Chapter 5

One
Hammered Work

The menorah was completely unique among the implements of the tabernacle in that it alone was to be of "one hammered work" (*miksheh*). From its base to its flowers, the lampstand was to be hammered from one gold ingot, not constructed of many segments, soldered or otherwise pieced together. The millions of molecules of gold that were to comprise the menorah were to be poured from the refiners fire in one ingot that was subsequently hammered into the desired shape. There was to be no division or plurality in the pure menorah.

ONENESS IN GOD

This feature of the menorah is a profound lesson both to Israel and to the church. It speaks first of the oneness of God. The first and greatest of all biblical statements (commandments) is this: "Hear, O Israel, the Lord our God, the Lord is one." This is the *Shema*[1] of Jewish tradition that is first and foremost a declaration of the uniqueness of God. He is wholly other: "Who is like you, O Lord, among the gods?"[2] sang Israel at the Reed Sea. "There is none like you," David exclaimed.[3] There is literally nothing to which God can be compared. His attributes are so far beyond human comprehension that many theologians have posited that he can be described only in terms of what he is not, not in terms of what he is.

The *Shema*, declaring the absolute oneness of God that allows for no plurality of being or substance, is the cornerstone of all biblical faith, the preeminent precept of God's instruction for man (the Torah). At the same time, the *Shema* is a statement of the unity of God. The final word of this declaration is *'echad* (one). The word *'echad*, however, stresses unity more than singularity. It is true that God is one; however, his oneness is that of a composite unity. The ancient sages of Israel understood this unity to be that of cohesion between the Creator and his Word and Spirit. The *Zohar*, the twelfth-century compilation of ancient concepts of Jewish mystical understanding, was not hostile to this concept of trinity (tri-unity), "since by its speculations regarding the father, the son, and the spirit it evolved a new trinity."[4] The *Zohar* taught that God is a composite unity of Father and King, Son (referred to in rabbinic writings as *Metatron*, the Angel of the Lord, and in the *Targumim* as *Memra*, the Word), and the Holy Spirit: "Thus are the three Spirits united in one. The Spirit which is downwards, who is called the Holy Spirit; the Spirit which is in the middle pillar, who is called the Spirit of Wisdom and of Understanding. . . . The upper Spirit is hidden in secret; in him are existing all the holy Spirits . . . and all that is light."[5] It also correctly answers the question of how three can be one: "How can they [the three] be One? Are they verily One, because we call them One? How Three can be One, can only be known through the revelation of the Holy Spirit."[6] The mystery of the *'echad* in Deity is revealed only by the Holy Spirit.[7] The composite oneness of God is absolute. There is no plurality in God.

The unity within deity was described by Jesus himself. Much to the consternation of his fellow Jews, he declared, "I and the Father are one."[8] Then he said rather matter-of-factly, "He who has seen me has seen the Father."[9] The stumbling stone upon which the first century leadership of Israel and the majority of subsequent Jewish people have fallen is the question of the deity of Jesus.[10] "How can a man become God?", they have wondered, equating the assertion of Jesus' deity with polytheism and as such an affront to Israel's preeminent commandment. It is an absolute truth that no man could ever hope to become God; however, it is also true that God can do anything he pleases, including become man. The real question for Israel and the world is, however, how and why God became the man Jesus, not how a man named Jesus became God.

The answer is in the Christian teaching that the Word of God, who proceeded from the Father before all creation[11] and was the agent of all creation,[12] chose to become incarnate as Jesus of Nazareth. The Word who was equal with God emptied himself of that equality[13] in order to become man and therefore less than divine–indeed, less than the angels–so that he could effect human redemption. This concept in no way projects the creation or manifestation of a second God based on the concepts of polytheism, as both Jewish and Christian scholars of the past and present have suggested. The manifestation of multiple persons within the one being of substance called God is a teaching that is solidly grounded in the church's Hebraic heritage.

Both Jewish and Christian scholars have asserted that the concept of the deity of Jesus is a Gentile dogma, derived from eastern mystery religions or from European polytheism. The truth is, however, that it is established on the clear teaching of Jewish scholars–namely, Jesus himself and his apostles. Since the end of the first century of the common era, rabbinic Judaism has appropriated to itself the right to speak for all of Jewry; however, in the days of Jesus, their antecedents, the Pharisees, were but one of a large number of sects of Judaism–and likely a minority, at that. None of the sects of that day could speak for all of Judaism; therefore, the opinions of one group were as viable as that of any other. To this day, Christianity is essentially a school of Jewish thought. The divine nature of Jesus, then, is also a Jewish teaching, formulated by the Jewish apostles and elders of the earliest church. It proceeds from Jewish thought and is based on the traditions of Jewish prophets and sages.

UNITY AND LIGHT

God is one, a unity in perfect cohesion, an eternal overlapping of attributes and wills both parallel and congruent. There is not the slightest discontinuity between the persons of God. The concord between Father, Son, and Holy Spirit is perfect. They are indeed a tri-unity. It is this total lack of friction and division that permits the triune God to emit the pristine light of the divine Presence that enshrouds the eternal Father in unapproachable glory and extends forth to lighten the universe, bringing the love and sustenance of God to created man.

The very essence of deity is revealed in the material creation.[14] The absolute unity of God in three persons is manifest in the material creation in light itself, the preeminent symbol for God. The pure, white light of the sun appears to be absolutely uniform; however, when passed through a prism, it is manifest to be composed of three colors of equal length in the spectrum of light: red, yellow, and blue. The rest of the colors of the rainbow result from the overlapping of these three primary colors. Light, then, is not merely one; it is three in one. Equal amounts of red, yellow, and blue blend together into one to make pure white light.

That the menorah was of one piece underscores the idea of oneness, both in God and in the company of his people, Israel, and of the church. At the time that Israel was commissioned and equipped to be God's light to the nations, they came together to be in one mind and one accord in one place. The sages have suggested that when Israel departed from Egypt, they were a divided, fragmented people. This is proven from the scriptural record that "Israel [singular] journeyed [plural] and camped [plural]."[15] When Israel reached Sinai, however, it was said that "Israel [singular] camped [singular]."[16] It was in this condition that Israel received the fullest disclosure of the Word and will of God in the form of the Ten Commandments. It is only in a condition of oneness that a people is able to receive clear enlightenment and then to manifest that light to others. So it was with Israel. When they were in the cohesion of biblical unity, they received divine insight from God and then became a light to the nations by reflecting God's light in their lifestyles and in their teaching.

ONE LORD, ONE FAITH

Jesus prayed for such a quality of unity among his disciples, the church, requesting of the Father during his Gethsemane experience "that they may be one, even as we are one."[17] The quality of unity that Jesus sought for his disciples was to parallel the absolute unity that he and his Father had shared from eternity past. They were not to be poured into a mold or stamped in a die to achieve complete uniformity. They were to be smelted together by the fiery Holy Spirit into one *gestalt* composed ultimately of millions of particles (individuals). In the composite unity of the menorah each of the molecules of gold has the potential to radiate and reflect the light. So it was with the church as God's light in the world. The entire corporate body of the church was the light of the world; however, each individual member of that body was also called to be a light, a mini-menorah as it were, reflecting God's grace to the world through their way of life infused with the Holy Spirit. When believers are connected to the Word of God, to Jesus, who is God's Light, and when they permit the Holy Spirit to purify them and fill them with the oil of his gladness, then they will be lights in a world of darkness.

Just as the menorah featured many decorations and distinctive parts yet remained one piece of gold, so the body of Christ is one, manifesting itself in a diversity of expressions. The unity of which the Holy Spirit is the agent[18] is the cohesiveness that binds the millions of molecules of pure gold together into one ingot that then radiates forth the light of the world, the pure, hammered, one-piece menorah. Jews have correctly understood unity to be cohesion of diverse elements while Christianity has erroneously viewed unity as uniformity, a sameness enforced by credalism.

Paul underscored the parallel between the unity of God and that of the church when he unequivocally declared that there is "one Lord, one faith, and one baptism."[19] Then he demonstrated how there could be one Lord manifest through one religion (faith) into which believers were initiated by one immersion: "One God and Father of all, who is above all and in you all." It was for this reason that the apostle encouraged the church to "endeavor to keep the unity of the Spirit in the bond of peace."[20] The unity that the apostle promoted was a unity of the Spirit, not a spirit of unity. It is possible for men of various associations to have a spirit of unity (sports teams, labor unions, political parties); however, the unity destined to characterize the church can be achieved only through the agency of the Holy Spirit. Christian unity must be the Holy Spirit's unity.

Paul further explained the nature of this ideal unity in the church: "So we, who are many, are one body in Christ, and individually we are members one of another."[21] The many-membered body of the Messiah must achieve *'echad* parallel with that in Deity. The oneness of God's congregation must be a reflection of God's oneness, fulfilling Jesus' final prayer.[22]

THE DARKNESS OF SCHISM

Division produces and reinforces spiritual darkness

because it creates an atmosphere that is hostile toward the manifestation of light. Such has been the case in most of ecclesiastical history. The church gave birth to the division monster by separating itself from Jews and Judaism. Beginning at the end of the first century and increasing to almost total separation in the fourth century, the proto-schism separated church from synagogue and fostered the dynamic of division within the church, a pattern that has been repeated *ad infinitum, ad nauseum*. A spirit of division was manifest in the church, and it would replicate itself in an unending virus of confusion, internecine strife, even self-consuming mayhem.

Today Christianity is perhaps the most divided religion in the world. Why? Because it founded its own self-identity upon division–its separation from Judaism. Since the fourth century, Christianity has largely defined itself as "non-Jewish." In reaction, Judaism has seen itself as "non-Christian." This schism between Christianity and Judaism has been unhealthy for both communities, but much more detrimental to Christianity. Wrenched from the moorings of its Jewish heritage, the church was set adrift in a maelstrom of human traditions and even demonic doctrines that have sorely limited its effectiveness as a force for light in the world. Christianity has suffered most greatly from an identity crisis. It has been uncertain of its ancestry, its spiritual patrimony, and its divine destiny as "spiritual Israel."

Identity based in negation proceeds from darkness and misunderstanding. The division in Christianity, based on its separation from Judaism and its rejection of its Hebraic heritage, so dimmed the light of divine revelation that the church was inevitably plunged into the Dark Ages, the era when ignorance and superstition reigned supreme in Europe and unethical conduct of every imaginable type came to characterize Christianity. Only when men within the church began to react against the division of church and synagogue and to insist that Christian understanding be based on the Hebrew Scriptures–in the context of the history and culture of the Jewish people–did a renaissance of understanding and hope begin.

MELTED, POURED, HAMMERED

The process of fashioning the menorah involved the melting, pouring, and hammering of pure gold. This is a paradigm for the spiritual requirements for making God's light shine in man's world. Melting removes the vestiges of individuality and selfishness and produces a true oneness in which every particle becomes a part of the greater whole. As the heat of the fire dissolves all resistance to the intentions of the craftsman, so the fiery Holy Spirit consumes any spiritual reluctance toward his purposes. The extreme heat of the liquefying fire is uncomfortable, to be sure; however, it is absolutely necessary that the gold be taken from its comfort zone into a true liquidity that is prepared and submitted to the molding of the Spirit. The heat forces the gold into oneness that can then be molded and hammered into a unified menorah of light.

Molding requires that the liquefied gold be poured out. In order to be conformed to the image of God's Son[23] so that they truly become the light of the world, believers must be poured out in complete abandon to the will and Word of God. In this state, they readily flow into the most inaccessible recesses of God's mold, fulfilling his design for their lives. When believers are daily transformed by the renewing of their minds,[24] their malleability to the Holy Spirit's purposes is maintained. Allowing oneself to be poured out in this manner is a supreme act of faith, a total commitment to God's will: "Not my will, but yours be done." Only when the church is poured out in complete submission to God's will is the unity achieved that produces light.

After the gold is molded, it must be hammered, subjected to the incessant beating process that stretches and adds detail and definition to its appearance. The continuing and repetitious pounding of God's Word gradually and systematically pressures believers into the Artisan's designed shape. The Word of God is indeed, "like a fire . . . like a hammer that breaks . . . into pieces."[25] It is the hammer of God's Word that divides and discerns the intents of the heart,[26] applying the gentle, but increasing pressure that forms the gold into the final image of the Living Menorah who then shines forth his light through that form. It fashions the individual particles of gold that have been melted, poured, and molded into the intricately detailed design that brings the one menorah's awe-inspiring light into the world.

When the melting, pouring, and hammering of the menorah is completed, it is fully capable of reflecting God's light and awaits only the introduction of oil into its lamps and the addition of the divine fire to make it God's light. Likewise only when God's people have become fully unified and have received the fullness of the Spirit in their lives, can they can fully become the light of the world.

REKINDLING THE UNITY LAMP

The renewal of the Holy Spirit in the church has fostered a spirit of restoration that has included efforts at rapprochement with Judaism and the Jewish people. In what has often been and remains a painful, hammering process, Christians have repented for the sins of their spiritual fathers against the Jewish people and against Judaism itself. This effort to heal the proto-schism has been healthy and life-giving for Christianity, for only when the root of division is removed can true unity emerge. Christianity will continue to find unity only to the degree that it restores its own Hebraic heritage. It will become one body again and will then enlighten the world only when it becomes the one hammered work, the divine menorah.

The light of the world must be one light raised upon a menorah of one hammered work, a body of people held in the cohesion of biblical unity. "If we walk in the light as Christ is in the light, we have fellowship with one another, and the blood of Jesus his Son cleanses us from all sin."[27] Only then will the church become God's lamp and man's light.

[1] *Shema* (hear) is the first word of the commandment, "Hear, O Israel, the Lord our God is one Lord."

[2] Exodus 15:11, New Revised Standard Version.

[3] Psalm 86:8.

[4] *Encyclopaedia Judaica*, Vol. 12, p. 261.

[5] *Zohar*, vol. 3, p. 26, quoted in Hirsch Prinz, *The Great Mystery: How Can Three Be One* (Cincinnati: M.L.O.), p. 27-28.

[6] *Zohar*, vol. 2, p. 43.quoted in Hirsch Prinz, overleaf, p. 18.

[7] 1 Timothy 3:16; 1 Corinthians 2:10.

[8] John 10:30.

[9] John 14:9, New King James Version.

[10] 1 Peter 2:8.

[11] John 13:3; 16:27.

[12] Colossians 1:16; John 1:3.

[13] Philippians 2:6-8.

[14] Romans 1:20.

[15] Exodus 17:1.

[16] Exodus 19:2.

[17] John 17:21-22.

[18] Ephesians 4:3.

[19] Ephesians 4:5.

[20] Ephesians 4:3.

[21] 1 Corinthians 10:17, New Revised Standard Version.

[22] John 17:21-22.

[23] Romans 8:29.

[24] Romans 12:2.

[25] Jeremiah 23:29.

[26] Hebrews 4:12.

[27] 1 John 1:7, New King James Version.

Chapter 6

Clear, Consecrated Oil

The menorah is of profound significance in and of itself. In order for it to produce illumination, however, it must have oil. The people of Israel were commanded, therefore, to bring "clear oil of beaten olives for the light so that the lamps may be kept burning continually."[1] In the wilderness sanctuary, this oil was to be of the finest quality, perfectly clear and free from all impurities. Olives were gently crushed in a mortar, not in an olive press, and the collected oil was kept in special jars, each holding oil sufficient to light the menorah for one night. The oil had to be consecrated in a process that required one week of work that was considered a sacred task. Once the oil was prepared for the menorah, it could never be used for other purposes. It could not even come into contact with anything that was not consecrated.[2]

Israel's sacred task of providing clear, consecrated oil for the light of God's lamp was so important to the people that they actually came to think of themselves as the ideal olive tree itself which supplies fruit and at the same time is light for all men.[3] Perhaps this connection between the people and the olive tree originated in the very appearance of the tree itself. Each leaf of the olive tree is dark green on its upper surface, but it is covered with whitish scales on its underside. When the leaves are moved by the wind, a shimmering wave of light appears to radiate from the tree. The olive tree, therefore, is seen as a tree of light, a symbol of the people of Israel who were to be God's olive tree and his light.

Jeremiah confirmed this concept by describing Israel as an "olive tree, beautiful in fruit and form,"[4] perhaps because this chosen people shed light upon all.[5] Paul maintained this tradition in his teaching that Israel was a cultivated, and therefore productive, olive tree while the Gentiles were a wild, unproductive olive tree.[6] Israel had been subjected to the pruning hook of God's law, the Torah; consequently, they had brought forth fruit unto righteousness, a light to the nations. The nations that came to faith in Jesus had been grafted into God's family tree of salvation and covenant relationship, the good olive tree, where they had received the infusion of enriching sap from Israel's roots. The Gentiles contributed to the enlightenment of the world only because they had become a part of Israel, God's olive tree. They, too, had been commissioned with Israel's sacred task of being a tree of light, providing oil for the lamp.

Providing oil for the light is essential, because believers in God, both Jews and Christians, cannot be mini-menorahs that bear the light of God's Word unless they have the oil of God's Spirit in their vessels. While many have abundant anointing with the oil of gladness and shine forth God's light, some are little more than mantel decorations. They appear stately and beautiful, but they are not functional, for they have no oil in their lamps. Without the oil of the Spirit of revelation, they cannot be light bearers.

This condition is clearly illustrated in Jesus' parable about the end of the age when the kingdom of God would be like ten virgins, all of whom were overcome in slumber.

At midnight a cry was made: "Behold, the bridegroom is coming; go out to meet him!"[7] At that shocking moment, all the kingdom arose and trimmed their lamps. This metaphor indicates that before the Messianic Age, a great awakening will occur. All the kingdom of believers will be trimming their lamps, a symbol for searching God's Word. Some, however, will find the task fruitless because they lack the oil of the Holy Spirit in their lamps. According to this parable, virtually all of those under God's dominion are in a state of slumber. Half of God's people, however, have an even more dreadful condition: they have no oil in their lamps.

This parable was given by Jesus to underscore the fact that each believer's individual menorah (the lamp of God's Word) must also be filled with the oil that allows the lamp to illuminate their path. This oil is the Holy Spirit, the anointing of God's presence that brings understanding and wisdom. The letter of the Word kills; however, the Spirit gives life.[8] It is essential that the Word of God be continually activated by the anointing of the Spirit's oil. David spoke thus of the need for this continual refreshment of anointing: "I have been anointed with fresh oil."[9]

In the ancient sanctuary, oil served two primary purposes: anointing and the production of light. The anointing oil, like the light oil, was specially formulated and consecrated. It featured the blending of pure oil with aromatic spices. When this oil was applied, it signaled God's approval upon men and their efforts. The delightful fragrance of the anointing oil served as a model for the pleasant state that is manifest when believers dwell together in unity.[10] Light and anointing go hand in hand. Without the anointing of the Holy Spirit that brings the pure oil of divine revelation into the lives of God's lamp, there can be no illumination. Even Jesus himself, the very Light of the world, was anointed with the Spirit in fulfillment of Isaiah's prophecy.[11] When he began his ministry, he went forth "in the power of the Spirit."[12] It is the Spirit's oil that provides both the sweetness of anointing and the light of insight and understanding.

Parallel with the fragrance of the anointing oil was the specially formulated incense that was burned upon the golden altar. The incense and the light from the menorah functioned together, for Israel was commanded concerning both בְּהַעֲלֹתְךָ (b'ha'alotekah), literally, "When you raise," or "When you cause to ascend." Israel was to raise both light and incense, to cause both to ascend together before God. Together light and incense form a profound unity that is both enlightening and a sweet savor.[13]

In order to bring forth God's kingdom on earth, both Jews and Christians must be anointed with the oil of joy in the *Ruach HaKodesh* (the Holy Spirit), so that their lamps manifest the light of the *Shekhinah*, God's Eternal Presence. And, they must do so in the same way in which ancient Israel accomplished the task, with "beaten olive oil." There are no shortcuts to obtaining the clear, consecrated oil that illuminates the menorah. Only through consecration and dedication to God can one be anointed with the oil of joy that produces spiritual light. Becoming God's lamp and man's light is no simple task!

[1] Leviticus 24:2, New American Standard Version, 1995 edition.

[2] Rudolph Brasch, *The Judaic Heritage* (New York: David McKay Co., 1969), p. 313.

[3] Edwin R. Goodenough, *Jewish Symbols in the Greco-Romans Period* (New York, Pantheon Books, 1953), IV, p. 89.

[4] Jeremiah 11:16, New American Standard Version, 1995 edition.

[5] *Shmot Raba* 36,1.

[6] Romans 11:24.

[7] Matthew 25:6.

[8] 2 Corinthians 3:6.

[9] Psalm 92:10.

[10] Psalm 133:1.

[11] Luke 4:18; Isaiah 61:1.

[12] Luke 4:14.

[13] Edwin R. Goodenough, IV, p. 91.

Chapter 7

The Light
Motif

The very first act in the creation of the present universe came with God's spoken Word: "Let there be light."[1] Suddenly in the universal darkness, light sprang forth, overwhelming the void of the formless universe with the pristine brightness of eternal glory. It is profoundly significant that the very first thing that God created was light. In a measure the light that radiated forth was the result of God's separating from himself a part of his very essence, the Person of his Word. The manifestation of God's Word always produces light,[2] a light that "penetrates to all degrees, from the lowest degree of natural, to the highest degree of spiritual light, and all that is light is united in him, who is light."[3]

God knew that light was essential to all that he would subsequently create. Light is life, and life is light. First, the life of God in the person of his Word became the agent from which light emerged, as the apostle John declared: "In him was life, and the life was the light of men."[4] Light, the substance of life, is the one element without which life cannot exist. All plant and animal life is wholly dependent upon the life-giving properties of the light that God spoke into existence through his Word.

Following the completion of this act of creation, "God saw the light that it was good."[5] The sages of Israel have expanded upon the Hebrew phrase אֶת־הָאוֹר (*et ha-or*)–here translated "the light"–noting that when the numerical equivalents of the Hebrew letters for this phrase are totaled, the sum is 613, the exact number of commandments in the Torah (the Pentateuch). Using this analysis, they have suggested that the light that pervaded the universe for the first three of creation's days–before the formation of the sun, moon, and stars–was the light of the supernal Torah, God's Word.

Light is equated with both knowledge and wisdom in Scripture. For this reason, the menorah speaks of enlightenment–learning, understanding, and reason–the light of knowledge that makes life meaningful and fulfilling. Light also speaks of wisdom in all of its forms. The fact that the menorah is made from one solid piece of gold and not of pieces soldered together reveals the truth that all wisdom is from one Source. Judaism recognizes the central shaft and its lamp as revealing both God and the Torah, the source of wisdom. The other six lamps, therefore, are oriented toward the center lamp to confirm the fact that all intellectual disciplines must serve the Word of God and its study.[6]

The menorah demonstrates that knowledge is not the exclusive possession of an elite, exclusive society, but is available to all men. The menorah's light is manifest in the diversity of seven lamps, indicating that while the light is not limited to a single channel, it is also not restricted to a single recipient. All men have the capacity to receive light and to reflect light. All that is needed is connection to the source of the light, the Living Menorah himself.

Light is more than mere understanding, however. "It is movement in that organic connotation which characterizes all processes of organic, vital, and spiritual development. Light illuminates life and also activates it; these two functions make light the metaphor of both cognition and the pulsating joy of living . . . the feeling of awareness of blossoming life."[7] Light leads to cognition and action as the spirit gives insight and wisdom and at the same time spurs man to moral volition and accomplishment.[8]

How sweet is the enlightening knowledge of God's Word. "Truly light is sweet,"[9] Solomon said. "The little scroll . . . tasted as sweet as honey in my mouth,"[10] John observed, as had Ezekiel before him.[11] The unfolding of God's Word gives light, providing insight to the most inexperienced.[12] It is the fullest disclosure of God's light that brings life. In Jewish tradition, light also speaks of joy and gladness. The happiness that the world pursues relentlessly to the point of exhausting all its energies and resources is the simple light of God's countenance. True happiness is knowing God and fulfilling his Word in a lifestyle that brings honor to him. It is the "inexpressible joy"[13] that fills one with glory when he sees and responds to the illumination of God's Word, when one accepts the Messiah as God's salvation.

The Hebrew Scriptures also use the words *lamp* and *light* to speak metaphorically of "the source of life and growth, of unfolding and flowering, of undisturbed progress."[14] Job recalled the time when God's lamp shown above his head and he walked through darkness aided by God's light.[15] He affirmed that God delivers from the path to the grave those who mend their ways and look to the light so that they may be illuminated by the light of life.[16] In Esther's day, despite the threat of genocide, there was light and joy for the Jews.[17] Scripture also equates the extinguishing of the light with the end of happiness.[18] For the righteous, however, there is the light of resurrection: "Your dead will live; their bodies will rise. You who dwell in the dust, wake up and shout for joy. Your dew is like the dew of [light]; the earth will give birth to her dead."[19] The Messiah's coming will emit the universal burst of light that will awaken the dead and bring forth the resurrection: "For as lightning that comes from the east is visible even in the west, so will be the coming of the Son of Man."[20]

Paul declared that the Heavenly Father dwells in light which no man can approach,[21] a light that envelops his essence so that he is eternally unknown, unrevealed, and incomprehensible. The only knowledge that man has of God is that which he has chosen to reveal through the person of the Word, his only begotten Son, and through the administration of his Spirit. John confirmed this truth: "No one has seen God at any time. The only begotten Son, who is in the bosom of the Father, he has declared him."[22] Peter also declared: "Holy men of God spoke as they were moved along by the Holy Spirit."[23]

According to John, then, it is uniquely the function of the Son of God, who became incarnate as Jesus of Nazareth, to reveal the Father.[24] As the fullest disclosure of the essence of God, Jesus put a face on the Father. Indeed, he is "the radiance of God's glory and the exact representation of his being."[25] Jesus is the fulfillment of David's prayer: "Lord, lift up the light of your countenance upon us."[26] The Son of God who was made flesh and tabernacled among men is the Word of God, the life force and essence of whom was the light of men.[27] In truth, Jesus was and remains "the light of the world,"[28] the living menorah. Even when God initiated creation by speaking the words, "Let there be light," he did so to indicate the coming days of the Messiah, of whom he also later spoke, "Arise, shine; for your light has come."[29]

In his incarnation, Jesus was the embodiment of the entire Torah, the only fully human being who ever fulfilled all of the Father's commandments. Because he never transgressed the law of God,[30] he was without sin. In him was no darkness at all: from him radiated only pristine light.[31] His entrance into every heart that has believed in him has brought light: clarity of purpose, focus of direction, insight of vision. His manifest presence always dispels darkness, gloom, and confusion. In every situation of darkness and every occasion of human brokenness,[32] he always commands: "Let there be light!"

Ultimately, the blessed Son of God will revisit planet earth to bring about a full restoration of all that was lost through man's fall. Yeshua ("salvation" in Hebrew) will appear the second time, not to bear the sins of the world but to effect complete salvation.[33] He awaits the time for the full restoration of the earth to the state of the Garden of Eden,[34] when, once again, the light that radiates from his presence will be the only light needed in the new heaven and the new earth. John described this event thus: "[the new Jerusalem] had no need of the sun, neither of the moon, to shine in it: for the glory of God did lighten it, and the Lamb is the light thereof."[35] The light that sprang forth from the voice of God in the beginning will be the same light that will illuminate the restored and renovated universe. The earth will be full of the knowledge of the Lord,[36] for the Word of God will permeate everything to such a degree that even on the pots and pans will be inscribed, "Holiness unto the Lord."[37] From the sublime to the mundane, everything will be set apart unto God.

In the end, as in the beginning, God will still be speaking through his Son, "Let there be light!", and God's Lamp will be man's light.

---

[1] Genesis 1:3.

[2] Psalm 119:130.

[3] Rabbi Tzvi Nassi, *How Can Three Be One?* (Cincinnati, Ohio: M.L.O.), p. 73

[4] John 1:4.

[5] Genesis 1:4.

[6] See the Wedsite: *www.torah.org.*

[7] S. R. Hirsch, *Selected Writings*, pp. 209-235, quoted at the Website: *http://members.tripod.com/~TheHope/menorah.htm*, p. 3.

[8] *Ibid.*

[9] Ecclesiastes 11:7.

[10] Revelation 10:10, New Revised Standard Version.

[11] Ezekiel 3:2-3.

[12] Psalm 119:130.

[13] 1 Peter 1:8, New King James Version.

[14] S. R. Hirsch, p. 3.

[15] Job 29:2-3.

[16] Job 33:28-30.

[17] Esther 8:16.

[18] Job 18:5; Proverbs 13:9; 20:20; 24:20.

[19] Isaiah 26:19, New International Version.

[20] Matthew 24:27, New International Version.

[21] 1 Timothy 6:16.

[22] John 1:18, New King James Version.

[23] 2 Peter 1:21.

[24] John 1:18.

[25] Hebrews 1:3.

[26] Psalm 4:6, New International Version.

[27] John 1:4.

[28] John 8:12.

[29] Rabbi Tzvi Nassi, *How Can Three Be One?* (Cincinnati, Ohio: M.L.O.), p. 73.

[30] 1 Peter 2:22; 1 John 3:4.

[31] 1 John 1:5.

[32] John 9:3.

[33] Hebrews 9:28.

[34] Acts 3:20-21.

[35] Revelation 21:23, King James Version.

[36] Isaiah 11:9.

[37] Zechariah 14:21.

Chapter 8

Man's Soul: God's Torch

Formed in God's image, man was intended by his Creator to dispel darkness.[1] Since God is light, it is perfectly understandable that man, the creation designed to reveal the image of the invisible God,[2] should be a channel of illumination to the whole of creation. This truth is asserted by Solomon in a somewhat cryptic statement that greatly adds to the understanding of God's purposes and methods for bringing light into the world. Translated variously as, "The spirit of man is the candle of the Lord,"[3] and, "The lamp of the Lord searches the spirit of a man,"[4] the Hebrew of this text simply declares, "A lamp of God, the soul of man."[5] This can be interpreted in two ways: "The lamp of God [enlightens] the soul of man," and "The soul of man [is] God's lamp." Both ideas are pregnant with meaning.

It is indeed the light of God that makes man a living soul. The simple soul (life) of man is in Hebrew the *nephesh,* the same term used to describe the life of other animals.[6] The living soul is the *neshamah,* the "breath of life" which God himself breathed into Adam's nostrils. It is the living soul, vivified by the very breath of God, that is enlightened by a spark of the Divine. The living soul expanded the dimension of life, for God's lamp is the light of man's soul.

The sages of Israel have also noted an anomaly in the Hebrew text of the account of creation that further confirms this truth. When Scripture speaks of God's creation of the beasts of the field and birds of the air, it uses the Hebrew word יֵצֶר (*yitzer*, formed). When it speaks of man's creation, however, it prefixes the word יֵצֶר with an extra י (*yod*), so that the word for "formed" in relationship to man is יִיצֶר. Some have speculated that the extra *yod* represents the introduction of the first letter of the Tetragrammaton, the Ineffable Name of God, into the act of creating man. The very Hebrew text, therefore, proclaims that God was doing something extraordinary when he created man in his image.

God's breathing the breath of life into Adam so that he became a "living soul" ignited the flame of illumination in the "earth being."[7] The spirit of man, the seat of human intellect and the power of reason, is the one element that distinguishes man from the rest of the earthbound creatures and indeed gives him dominion over them.[8] It is the factor in the totality of man's being that causes him to be created in God's image.[9]

Man's physical features are not what makes him in the image of God. Otherwise the great apes would share that image. In reality, God has no physical appearance, and the various anthropomorphisms and theriomorphisms that are ascribed to him in Scripture merely enable men to understand God more clearly and to relate to him more fully. God is spirit,[10] ultimately unfathomable, unquantifiable, incomprehensible,[11] and unapproachable.[12] What man understands about God is only what God has chosen to reveal to him. The enlightenment that man has experienced is infinitesimal compared to the infinite light of Deity.

The act of breathing the "breath of life" into Adam served a greater purpose than mere vivification of his lifeless body. It infused in him a spark of the Divine that lit the first human torch to radiate the image and likeness of God to all creation. The intelligence, the power of reason, and the conscience that were embodied in the soul of man became the light of the world. It was with the spirit of man to which the Holy One communicated his good pleasure and upon which he showered his very essence, pure love.

MAN'S SPIRIT–A CHANNEL OF ILLUMINATION

Elihu, the upstart, but true friend of Job, stated this idea succinctly: ". . . there is a spirit in man: and the breath of the Almighty gives him understanding."[13] Literally in Hebrew, this statement declares that the *ruach* (spirit) in man is given understanding by the *neshamah* (breath) of the Almighty. The knowledge that God imparts to man is the illumination of man's spirit. All understanding is conveyed by the agency of God's Spirit. There is no dichotomy between "spiritual" knowledge and "secular" understanding. Everything is theological and spiritual, as the Jewish people have observed.[14] Since all knowledge and understanding is the infusion of insight from the Spirit of God to the spirit of man, man has no occasion to boast in his own inventiveness, creativity, or intellectual prowess. All illumination of the human spirit, whether for spiritual understanding or material insight, is a gift of God's grace.

This truth sheds light on Joel's prediction that in the last days God would pour out his Spirit upon *all* flesh.[15] All human beings are impacted by the outpouring of God's knowledge. Included among them are those sons and daughters who prophesy and declare the works of God.[16] This concept also underscores the accuracy of Daniel's statement that at the end of the age *knowledge* would be increased.[17] Man's intellect has appreciated not one degree since Adam. Indeed, with all of modern technology, marvels of the ancient world have not even been understood, much less replicated. It is *knowledge* that has been increased in the modern and post-modern worlds, and it is knowledge that continues to be multiplied exponentially as the Messianic Era approaches. God illuminates the spirits of men with the flashes of insight that produce the *"eureka"* experience. The truth that all knowledge is from God's light, not man's might, is confirmed by the synchronization of knowledge in which increased insight in any particular discipline invariably comes to unrelated and unconnected people at the same time. Inventive genius results from God's inspiring light.

That the spirit of man is a spark of the Divine to which God communicates his light is confirmed in the fact that when the entity of man dies, the body returns to the dust, but "the spirit returns to God who gave it."[18] Each individual's allotment of the power of reason and conscience is directly from God and returns to God when that individual's time on earth expires. The power of reason, accompanied by the right of choice (free will), demonstrates man's reflection of God's image, God's positive gift to every human being.

God's deposit into every human being is the spark of the divine that draws men toward God. It is reflected in the writing of God's ethical demands on the hearts of men so that their consciences either condemn or excuse them.[19] The sages have characterized this concept as the *"yetzer tov,"* the inclination toward good that is inherent in all men. They also point out that a *yetzer hara*, an evil inclination, tends to encourage evil in men's hearts. And, the battle rages, even as the apostle asserted.[20] The spark of the divine enlightens men's hearts, wooing them toward God. The Father's Spirit draws men toward Messiah, generating faith in their hearts through the agency of the living Word[21] that illuminates their lives. Evil, however, is always present[22] to subvert men's hearts and lead them astray.

Because man is a free moral agent with the power of

choice, the potential is always present for the choice of evil. Evil, however, is the perversion of goodness, for in all good is the potential for abuse that takes the good outside the parameters that God has established for its enjoyment. Evil, then, is the absence of light. When the light within one becomes darkness, "how great is that darkness!"[23] When men know the illumination of God in their spirits and turn from that light, either by claiming that it has proceeded from their own intellect or by worshiping the creation rather than the Creator, they become reprobates, black holes from which no light can escape.[24]

The spirit of man is God's lamp, the channel through which divine insight is manifest. All knowledge that enlightens man is from God. It is the lampstand on which God kindles the fire of his *Shekhinah* to produce illumination for life and peace. Because man is endowed with a living soul, he is in reality God's lamp, the vehicle of God's light both to himself and to others.

MECHANICS OF LIGHT-BEARING

How does man become a vehicle for light? With their focus on the mystical, Chassidic Jews have analyzed this process, considering the various elements of the menorah–its fire and light.[25] They note that the lampstand is a continuum of three essential parts: oil, wick, and vessel. The oil is fed from the vessel through the wick to the flame. It is through the interaction of these three elements that light is generated and sustained.

Neither the wick nor the oil could independently produce the efficient flame of the lamp. An ignited wick would flare up, only to be momentarily consumed. Olive oil alone would be difficult to ignite and would not sustain a flame. When the wick channels oil from the vessel to the flame, however, the three units together produce a steady, controlled light. Though the wick and the oil are combustible, unless they function together with the vessel, a sustained flame that can produce illumination is impossible.

This lesson from the material menorah speaks volumes of spiritual understanding. First, the three physical elements that produce the menorah's light can be compared to the three persons in God: Father, Word, and Spirit. The Father is the vessel, the container of everything that is God. The Word is the wick, that which became material in the incarnation so that the light might be fully disclosed. The oil is the Holy Spirit, the one who anoints and who sustains the light. This triunity functions so as to translate the unapproachable light of infinite grace into a form that illuminates mankind.

The material lamp also is revealed in the interaction that uses man to bear God's light. The soul of man becomes the lamp of God enlightening the world with his Divine light when the fuel of the light, God's Word, is manifest through a physical body (the wick) to channel the oil and convert it into the illuminating flame. The Word of God (manifest in the Torah) represents the sum total of divine wisdom and truth; however, for that Word to enlighten the world, it must be studied, comprehended, taught, disseminated, and inculcated into the lives of others. God has also designed it that the divine oil of his Word does not produce illumination without the wick of human agency. Faith comes from hearing the Word of God, but hearing is impossible without a preacher.[26]

In like manner, man can produce but a momentary, self-consuming flash of light without God's Word. A life void of the Word of God that is both believed and practiced is incapable of sustaining light. Like a wick without oil, man may generate flashes of ecstatic personal insight, the stuff of existentialism; however, these exercises shed no enduring light into the world.

If human lives (souls) are to be God's menorah, they

must allow the oil of divine revelation from God's Word to combust in their physical entity, producing the good works that Jesus said would illuminate the world. When men, like the wick, are saturated with a steady supply of the oil of insight from the Holy Spirit, the flame that results is luminous and enduring. Ironically, as the physical oil both preserves the existence of the wick and through it produces light, so the Word of God both preserves man and through him illuminates the world.

The flame itself also reveals man's interaction with the Divine. "The 'wick' is both prison and liberator for the flame, both tether and lifeline. . . . a relationship with God that is characterized by two conflicting drives, a yearning to come close coupled with a commitment to draw back. . . . The flame surges upwards, as if to tear free from the wick and lose itself in the great expanses of energy that gird the heavens. But even as it strains heavenward, it is already pulling back, tightening its grip on the wick and drinking thirstily of the oil in the lamp . . . it is this tension of conflicting energies, this vacillation from being to dissolution and back again, that produces light."[27]

In man, as God's lamp, the polarity between being attracted into union with the Divine and maintaining the corporeality of humanity converge in a flame that illuminates its surroundings with a godly light. The ideal that is luminous is not to escape into the Divine in some ecstatic, other-worldly existence; it is to infuse the human spirit with the Divine glory in acts of measured obedience to God's imperatives. Fulfilling God's Word through the agency of the indwelling Holy Spirit produces that spiritual light.

[1] Rudolph Brasch, *The Judaic Heritage* (New York: David McKay Co., 1969), p. 309.
[2] Romans 1:19.
[3] Proverbs 20:27, King James Version.
[4] Proverbs 20:27, New International Version.

[5] Proverbs 20:27, literal translation from Hebrew.

[6] Job 12:10: "The soul [*nephesh*] of every living thing."

[7] Adam in Hebrew is from *adamah*, meaning earth or dirt.

[8] Genesis 1:26.

[9] Genesis 1:27.

[10] John 4:24.

[11] Romans 11:33.

[12] Job 11:17.

[13] Job 32:8.

[14] Marvin R. Wilson, *Our Father Abraham: Jewish Roots of the Christian Faith* (Grand Rapids: Wm. B. Eerdmans Publishing Company, 1989), p. 156.

[15] Joel 2:28a.

[16] Joel 2:28b.

[17] Daniel 12:4.

[18] Ecclesiastes 12:7.

[19] Romans 2:15.

[20] 2 Corinthians 10:5; Ephesians 6:12.

[21] Romans 10:17.

[22] Romans 7:21.

[23] Matthew 6:23, New International Version.

[24] Romans 1:28; Titus 1:16; Hebrews 6:4-6.

[25] This analogy is based on an analysis of the menorah by Rabbi Schneur Zalman of Liadi condensed for *Torah@Home*, published by Chabbad of Birmingham, Alabama, and distributed via e-mail.

[26] Romans 10:13-14.

[27] Rabbi Schneur Zalman, quoted in *Torah@Home*, 6-25-01.

Chapter 9

Israel: God's Menorah

The Jewish people see in the seven flames of the menorah the collective souls of Israel as God's light to the nations.[1] From the time he incorporated them as his chosen nation, God commissioned Israel to be the light of the world. "Keep therefore and do them; for this is your wisdom and your understanding in the sight of the nations, which shall hear all these statutes, and say, Surely this great nation is a wise and understanding people."[2] Israel was to model before the nations a lifestyle governed by God's instructions. The successful and blessed lives that they would live in obedience to the Word of God would enlighten the Gentiles and turn them to God. As they elevated the light of the menorah, Israel would also be exalted.[3]

Jewish tradition says, "God is the Light of the universe . . . yet he commands that a lamp be lighted to give light back to God. . . . So God has led Israel by his light, and in gratitude Israel is to give light in return. . . . The light of the menorah does not perish as must even the Temple, but in its continued burning symbolizes the fact that God's blessings endure forever for his children."[4] This concept suggests that the illumination that God gives to man is then reflected not only to the world but also to God himself. The grace of God that brings illumination is returned to God in the form of praise.[5]

Isaiah confirmed the nature of Israel's witness: " 'You are my witnesses,' declares the Lord, 'and my servant whom I have chosen, so that you may know and believe me and understand that I am he. Before me no god was formed, nor will there be one after me.'"[6] So that the nations of the world would believe that the Eternal alone is God, Israel was chosen to bear witness to this truth by manifesting a lifestyle of obedience to God's commandments that would make them a productive, successful people. Israel's faithfulness to God and their resultant blessing would be a radiant example to the world that would point beyond both the lampstand and the light to the Source of the light, to God himself.

The Talmud further clarifies Israel's commission to be a light unto the nations: "Israel said before God: 'Lord of the Universe, thou commandest us to illumine before thee. Art thou not light of the world, and with whom light dwelleth?' . . . 'Not that I require your light,' was the Divine reply, 'but that you may perpetuate the light which I conferred on you as an example to the nations of the world!' "[7] Israel understood, then, that God needed their light only as a means of perpetuating the Divine light that he had given to them to be an example to the nations.

RAISING THE LIGHT

Even the words of the commandment for lighting the menorah speak of Israel's being elevated so as to enlighten the Gentile world. The command is בְּהַעֲלֹתְךָ אֶת־הַנֵּרֹת (b'ha'alotecha et-ha-nerot), "When you raise the light."[8] Israel was designed to lift up God's fire upon a lampstand so it would give light to the household of humanity. They were not to hide, or lower, the light. They were to raise it, exalt it, make it glorious. Israel itself was elevated above the other nations of the world for the express purpose of raising the light: "For you are a holy people to the Lord your God, and the Lord has chosen you to be a people for himself, a special treasure above all the peoples who are on the face of the earth."[9] Israel was not exalted to the status of an elite super race; they were chosen in order to raise God's light. Israel was selected to be a demonstration of God's holiness. The *Zohar* declared that the menorah's wick is Israel, while its oil is the Torah and its light is the *Shekhinah*.[10]

Even when given the exquisite physical menorah and its glorious light, Israel looked beyond the living emblem and its radiant splendor to the Divine Light himself. They knew that their own radiance and that of the menorah were wholly dependent upon God, as the prophet declared: "Arise, shine; for thy light is come, and the glory of the Lord is risen upon thee."[11] Israel could arise to shine only because God's glorious light had risen upon them. Rabbi Yochanan observed that Israel declared before God, "We have made a menorah in the days of Moshe, and it went out; in the days of Shlomo, it went out. From now on we shall wait only for your light. As it is said, 'For with you is the source of life, and by your light shall we see light.' Likewise did God say, 'Arise, shine, for your light has come!' "[12]

Isaiah further spoke of God's selection of Israel to enlighten the world: "I, the Lord, have called you in righteousness; I will take hold of your hand. I will keep you and will make you to be a covenant for the people and a light for the Gentiles."[13] He further expanded upon this theme: "It is too small a thing for you to be my servant to restore the tribes of Jacob and bring back those of Israel I have kept. I will also make you a light for the Gentiles, that you may bring my salvation to the ends of the earth."[14] While both of these prophecies are ultimately Messianic predictions, they also apply to Israel, the corporate body of witnesses whom God chose to be his menorah light to the nations of the world and to bring his salvation to the ends of the earth.

In order to have a vehicle for the dissemination of his
light, God formed Israel according to the heavenly pattern to
be a menorah on which his light could be raised to radiate into
the world. Israel was not chosen because of their own great-
ness. Indeed, God expressly noted that he had called Israel
because they were "the fewest of all people."[15] God's intent
was to place his light in an insignificant, nomadic tribe and,
by illuminating their lives with the goodness of his Torah,
make them his menorah to the nations. In God's design, therefore, Israel was not an end in itself but a means to the end–
God's predetermined goal to cover the earth with his truth and
glory. Paul, the rabbi from Tarsus, noted this commission as it
was later manifest in those who had become a part of Israel
through faith: ". . . to make all men see what is the plan of the
mystery hidden for ages in God who created all things."[16] All
men were to be confronted with the illuminating mysteries of
God's Word through the agency of his chosen people.

THE TORAH–GOD'S LIGHT

While God has always radiated his light in the lives
of individuals, he needed a corporate vehicle to demonstrate the ultimate light of the Torah encapsulated in the
two greatest divine commands: "Love God" and "Love
man."[17] Love for God can be expressed individually; however, love for man can be manifest only in the context of
community. Indeed, even love for God must be manifest
by means of love for man as John asserted: "He who does
not love does not know God, for God is love. . . . If someone says, 'I love God,' and hates his brother, he is a liar;
for he does not love his brother whom he has seen, how
can he love God whom he has not seen?"[18]

The first five of the ten words at Sinai were designed
to instruct Israel how to love God with all their being. The
remaining words–along with their further explication in
other *mitzvot* (commandments) were designed to reveal to

Israel what it meant for man to love man–to love one's neighbor as himself. Such love is impossible without the aid of divine light through the Holy Spirit. Man's instinct for survival, especially in the fallen state of sin, tends toward idolatry–the worship of gods of money, power, pleasure–and toward narcissism. It also tends toward self-interest, self-indulgence, greed, hatred, and the elevation of class distinctions. Only when the love of God is reflected by the light of God's Word and Spirit[19] into men's lives are they able to love God totally and to love neighbor as self, even the neighbor in the far reaches of the global village. The evil inclination toward idolatry, greed, and self interest is overcome by the good inclination that is reinforced by the continual radiance of God's Spirit.

No individual is complete in himself. Man is designed by God to be gregarious. Isolationism is an aberration. Marriage is the first step toward God's design for corporate man. Then family further unfolds this plan, creating more opportunity for the expression of the light of love. Extended family further expands the corporate demonstration. Community gives a broadened opportunity for the manifestation of light, which then can be extended to the entire family of mankind.

BELIEVING OR DOING?

Another important factor in Israel's menorah status is that they are to enlighten the world by concrete action, not by abstract theory. They are not asked to affirm their beliefs: they are required to fulfill God's commandments. When God gave the Decalogue, Israel replied, "All that the Lord has said, we will do, and we will hear [intelligently],"[20] and in that order. They did not expect to understand the divine will first and then to do it. They committed themselves to doing it first and then striving to understand it. Much of God's perfect light for man is irrational to man. God's ways are often inscrutable. They can be understood only when they are experienced.

Those who refuse to do will never see.

Israel, therefore, has always been more concerned with doing than with believing. Faith is not mere intellectual assent to a divine premise. It is faithfulness, the act of walking out one's belief in concrete action. Orthodoxy, therefore, is not nearly as important as orthopraxy. Light is not just belief; it is good works.

Light is not, therefore, a product of what one believes. It is manifest in what one does. Ideas can be cold and clinical, jejune and lifeless. Theoreticians are often abstract and befuddled. Ideas and theories unfulfilled in concrete action are worthless mental gymnastics, void of light. More often than not abstract knowledge merely inflates the ego of its possessor,[21] leading him off into meaningless mental exercises that rarely provide illumination and frequently lead to darkness, opening the door to abject evil.

What was required of Israel, therefore, was dynamic modeling–demonstrating through lifestyle the practicality of divine imperatives. The Rabbi from Nazareth was himself approved of God by "doing good."[22] He emphasized this Hebraic truth to his disciples, declaring that their "good works" would be the light to bring God glory.[23] He further instructed them that they would *be witnesses* to him through their lifestyle, not that they would *bear witness* to him by their words.[24] Their Christian walk–their dynamic modeling of his teachings–would be the world's living witness. "Men will know you are my disciples," he told them, "if you have love one for another."[25] When the public observed the apostles' actions, they recognized immediately that they "had been with Jesus."[26] This is why these earliest Jewish believers in Jesus were commissioned to go into all the world and herald the good news of the emerging kingdom.

Jesus' disciples, however, merely perpetuated and extended Israel's commission to demonstrate his truth to the nations as the light of the world. As a matter of fact, the

Sanhedrin, the central seat of Jewish religious and juridical authority,[27] was considered to be the supreme concentration of Jewish wisdom and therefore to be the light of the world.[28] It was the Sanhedrin that established *halachah*, enlightening the way in which the Jewish people should walk. Jesus himself recognized the authority of this body to decide how Jews should conduct themselves[29] and instructed his disciples to do as they commanded.

The understanding that Israel was the light of the world was the driving force behind Israel's first missionary zeal. Missiology is not a Christian invention. It was in force long before the birth of Christianity. The Jews were engaged in the exercise of going into the world, preaching the kingdom of God, God's dominion over the affairs of men through his Torah. Inscribed above one of the arches leading from the temple complex were the words, "Go and make many disciples," words that Jesus repeated in the Great Commission.[30] The work of reflecting God's menorah, then, was much more for Israel than simple public witness. It involved the work of convincing and converting the heathen nations to the godly lifestyle that Judaism represented. Indeed, the road was paved for the expansion of Christianity throughout the Mediterranean basin and beyond by the missions of the Jews who earlier had borne the torch of God's truth among the nations.

For 3,500 years, Israel has continued to be God's lamp, man's light. Though many Christian theologians have posited that God rejected his ancient people in favor of the church, Paul strongly renounced this assertion: "God has not rejected his people whom he foreknew. . . . Did they stumble so as to fall beyond recovery? Not at all!"[31] Despite every genocidal attempt to snuff out their lives, Israel remains to this day God's Torah light to the nations, modeling the ethical conduct that God demands and serving as a material witness to God's immutability.[32]

[1] Isaiah 42:6; 49:6.

[2] Deuteronomy 4:6.

[3] *Midrash Rabbah*, Numbers 15:4.

[4] *Midrash Rabbah*, Numbers 15:5.

[5] This idea is clearly seen in the Greek text of the New Testament, where the word for grace, *charis*, is found in the word for gift, *charisma*, and in the word for thanksgiving, *eucharistia*. Grace flows from God to man. It is then transferred laterally to others through the gifting of the Holy Spirit. Finally, it returns to God in the form of thanksgiving and praise. (I am indebted to my close friend and colleague, Dr. Karl D. Coke, for the basis of this insight.)

[6] Isaiah 43:10, New International Version.

[7] Rudolph Brasch, *The Judaic Heritage* (New York: David McKay Co., 1969), p. 309.

[8] Numbers 8:1: Here the words בְּהַעֲלֹתְךָ אֶת־הַנֵּרֹת (*B'ha'alotecha et-haNerot*), rendered "When thou lightest the lamps" in the King James Version, are literally translated, "When you raise the light." The New International Version translates this phrase, "When you set up the lamps." In parallel passages in Exodus 25:37; 40:4, the words וְהַעֲלֵיתָ אֶת־נֵרֹתֶיהָ (*v'ha'aleat et-nerotyah*), rendered "and light the lamps thereof," are literally rendered "and raise light thereof."

[9] Deuteronomy 14:2, New King James Version.

[10] Nathan Ausubel, *The Book of Jewish Knowledge* (New York: Crown Publishers, 1964), p. 277.

[11] Isaiah 60:1.

[12] Eliyahu Kitov, *The Book of Our Heritage* (Jerusalem: Feldheim Publishers, 1968), p. 294.

[13] Isaiah 42:6, New International Version.

[14] Isaiah 49:6, New International Version.

[15] Deuteronomy 7:7.

[16] Ephesians 3:9, New Revised Standard Version.

[17] Matthew 22:37-40.

[18] 1 John 4:8, 20, New King James Version.

[19] Romans 5:5.

[20] Exodus 24:7, literal translation from Hebrew.

[21] 1 Corinthians 8:1.

[22] Acts 10:38.

[23] Matthew 5:16.

[24] Acts 1:8.

[25] John 13:35.

[26] Acts 4:13.

[27] Daniel Sperber, "History of the Menorah," *The Journal of Jewish Studies*, XVI, Nos. 3, 4, 1965, p. 153.

[28] Babylonian Talmud, *Bava Bathra* 5a.

[29] Matthew 23:2-3.

[30] Matthew 28:19.

[31] Romans 11:2 (New Revised Standard Version), 11:11 (New International Version).

[32] Malachi 3:6.

Chapter 10

You Are the Light of the World

When Jesus ordained his disciples as the world's light, he was operating in complete continuity with the heritage of his Jewish contemporaries. "Ye are the light of the world" was not a novel or revolutionary concept. Jesus was merely recommissioning his apostles with Israel's ancient enjoinder to be the light to the nations.

First, Jesus had identified himself personally and individually as the light: "I am the light of the world."[1] He had been declared to be the fulfillment of Isaiah's "light to the nations" prophecy at the time of his dedication. As Simeon, the aged priest, held the infant Jesus, he exclaimed, "For my eyes have seen your salvation which you have prepared before the face of all peoples, a light to bring revelation to the Gentiles, and the glory of your people Israel."[2] The living Menorah had come to bring light both to Israel and to the nations. Jesus, the perfect man, revealed to mankind not only what it meant to be fully divine but also what it meant to be fully human. The fullest essence of humanity was manifest in Jesus, the first time pure humanity had been seen since Adam's creation. Is it any wonder, then, that he was God's menorah. "As long as I am in the world, I am the light of the world,"[3] he emphatically declared.

Later, during his ministry, Jesus told his disciples that

what he had been individually, they were to be collectively and corporately. They were to be *to soma tou Christou*, the "body of Christ," a collective of individuals whose gifts and graces made them corporately what Jesus, in his incarnation, was personally. As the body of the Messiah, they were to be the light of the world.[4] Because he was returning to his Father, they would do even greater works than he had done.[5] They were to become God's menorah to the nations. Because they had come to faith in Jesus, they were to manifest the light by walking in a way pleasing to God, doing so solely on the basis of their faith in God. Paul lucidly expressed this truth thus: "You were once darkness, but now you are light in the Lord. Live as children of light (for the fruit of the light consists in all goodness, righteousness, and truth) and find out what pleases the Lord."[6] Peter noted that the Gentiles also had been called out of their darkness into God's marvelous light, thereby becoming a part of God's chosen nation so that they, along with Israel, might "proclaim [God's] mighty acts,"[7] thereby further illuminating the world.

Jesus used two metaphors to elucidate the way in which the light should radiate from his disciples. First, he declared that they were never to hide the light or consume it upon themselves. They, like Israel of old, were to raise the light, placing it atop a lampstand so that it could illuminate all. With the corporate consciousness of Israel and of his disciples focused on the menorah as the symbol of light and liberty to God's people, could his metaphorical reference have been to anything other than the menorah? Just as the menorah gave perpetual light signifying God's eternal presence among his people, so Jesus' disciples were to raise the light of God's Word for supernatural illumination of the entire world.

THE CITY ON A HILL

The second metaphor that Jesus employed was that of

a city positioned on a hill whose light cannot be hidden. This was, no doubt, a reference to Jerusalem–the city on the hill of Mount Zion. Jerusalem was the joy of the whole earth.[8] It was called Jerusalem the Golden after the light that radiated to the surrounding area from its golden stone. It was positioned in the heights so that the Jewish people always "went up" to Jerusalem.[9] Jewish tradition often referred

Topographical map of Jerusalem demonstrating the Hebrew letter *shin*, the first letter of God's name, *Shaddai*. (Photo prepared by Hammond, Inc, Maplewood, N.J.)

to the temple hill (Moriah) as "God's sacred mountain," to Jerusalem as the "Center of the Universe," and to the spring issuing from the temple mount as the future "River of Paradise," alongside which the leaves of the trees would not wither nor their fruit would not fail.[10]

Jerusalem was the city of the Great King,[11] the habitation of the Almighty,[12] the place where God had chosen to place his name.[13] Indeed, in the very topography of Jerusalem one can see the imprint of the Divine, for the valleys that circumscribe and intersect the holy city form the Hebrew letter שׁ (*shin*), the letter that has always stood for one of God's names, שַׁדַּי (*Shaddai*), among the Hebrew peoples. The *shin* literally means teeth, but it also graphically illustrates fire. One can even see the flames leaping up in this letter of the Hebrew alphabet. God, the consuming fire, is indeed *El Shaddai*, and his dwelling place is Zion–the mountain of Jerusalem, the people of Judah, and the congregation of Messiah.

Out of Jerusalem, God shines, for the Word of the Lord goes forth from Mount Zion illuminating the world.[14] Jerusalem was the place where God commanded Israel to worship

him continually.[15] It was the place where the menorah, the
eternal lamp, was to burn in his sanctuary before him forever.
The disciples readily understood this metaphor and eventually came to see themselves as a spiritual manifestation of
Jerusalem, the city of God. They were the Mount Zion, the
holy city, a habitation for God by the Spirit. "You have come
to Mount Zion and to the city of the living God, the heavenly
Jerusalem . . . to the general assembly and church of the first-
born who are registered in heaven,"[16] they claimed. The Jews
believed that the earthly Jerusalem was patterned after the
heavenly Jerusalem, God's abode. Likewise, the apostles
viewed themselves children of the Jerusalem above[17] so that
they, too, were a spiritual or heavenly Jerusalem.

The disciples were to take the menorah light that was
localized in Jerusalem and transport it into the entire earth.
They were to begin at Jerusalem, the light capital of the
world, and go to "Judea, Samaria, and the uttermost part of
the earth."[18] Like their ancestors, they were commissioned
to "go and make many disciples." They were to be the light
of the world, a spiritual city elevating the light in such a
way that it could not be hidden.

LIGHTING THE MENORAH

So that they could become the light of the nations and
fill Israel's commission fully, the earliest Jewish believers
in Jesus were immersed in the divine fire, the fiery Holy
Spirit.[19] As they gathered in one accord in Jerusalem on
the very day of Pentecost following Jesus' ascension, the
rushing wind of the Holy Spirit filled the room where they
were assembled, and tongues of fire sat upon each of them.
They began speaking in xenoglossy, languages with which
they were not familiar, so that people from all the nations
of the world who had gathered in the temple complex for
the second of Israel's annual pilgrimage festivals heard "the
wonderful words of God" in their own languages.[20] In a

repeat of the first Pentecost at Sinai, the Word of God went forth in fire. Literally, a human menorah was lit on that day with the fiery Holy Spirit, and their number multiplied exponentially as the light from that fire was shed abroad.[21]

The light of the spiritual city, however, was the Lamb of God. The Torah that had enlightened Israel became incarnate in Jesus, the Lamb of God who removes the sin of the world.[22] "This is my beloved Son,"[23] the Heavenly Father declared of him. The glory of the Father, the brightness and radiance of divine light, shone in the face of Jesus.[24] The body of Christ would, therefore, be the light of the world only as it became a lampstand to raise the person of the Light. Whereas the faith of Israel–and indeed of Jesus himself–had been Torah-centric, the faith of the restored congregation was to be Christocentric, for the living Christ was the Torah fully manifest. The life and light of the church was to be manifest only as it was connected to the source of the light, Jesus himself.

The earliest church took very seriously Jesus' commission to be the light of the world. After the door of faith was opened to the Gentiles in the supernatural event that lit the fire on the household of Cornelius,[25] the apostles dispersed from Jerusalem into various parts of the world, taking the gospel message with them. They fully understood that they had been commissioned as the body of the Messiah to continue the fulfillment of the Messianic commission to be the light of the nations. The menorah was to become more than a national symbol for Israel. It was to become the emblem of faith among all nations.

Paul assumed personal responsibility for enlightening the nations in the fulfillment of Isaiah's prophecy. "For so the Lord has commanded us, saying, 'I have set thee to be a light for the Gentiles, so that you may bring salvation unto the ends of the earth.'"[26] The Messianic commission was furthered through the men who were indwelled by the

Spirit of the Messiah, as the menorah incarnate filled his congregation with light and transformed them into a corporate living menorah. The church as a part of Israel was destined to be God's lamp and man's light.

A SMOKING WICK?

The sad truth, however, is that both the church and Israel have often failed miserably to be the light to the nations that God intended. Though given a perfect operating manual for illuminating behavior, the Jewish people all too often drifted into isolation, separatism, exclusivity, and elitism, qualities which were replicated centuries later in minute detail by the Christian church. The lamps of God's human menorah were often extinguished, and the menorah was befouled with multiple violations of the source of light, the Word of God.

Even in this condition, however, God never rejected either of his peoples, Israel or the church. The infidelity of some men never obviates God's fidelity to his beloved creation, mankind. "God's gifts and his call are irrevocable."[27] Graphic demonstrations of God's faithfulness to his covenant with Israel and the church are seen in the words of Isaiah: "A bruised reed he will not break, and a dimly burning wick he will not extinguish; he will faithfully bring forth justice. He will not be disheartened or crushed until he has established justice in the earth."[28] The term *bruised reed* projects a simple natural image of a reed that has been crushed; however, in juxtaposition with the phrase *dimly burning wick* it also suggests the idea of a damaged lampstand. In this prophetic word, it represents historical Israel as being a damaged menorah for a nearly extinguished light; however, the promise is that Israel would survive. The chosen people were chastized, but not destroyed; they were dimmed, but not extinguished.[29]

Jeremiah made a similar statement regarding Israel:

"The vessel he was making of clay was spoiled in the potter's hand, and he reworked it into another vessel, as seemed good to him."[30] Though the clay pot that the artisan was molding became marred in his hand, he did not discard it but rather reworked the same clay into another vessel that pleased him. God has always remained faithful to his promises to Israel and continues to work his vessel toward the goal of honor and light. He never gives up on his people!

What was said of Israel in the prophecies of Isaiah and Jeremiah can be applied equally to the body of Christ. The church has more often than not been a damaged menorah reed, a flickering, smoking wick, failing miserably in its commission to be the light of the world. God, however, has never given up on the church, any more than he has rejected his people Israel. With both peoples, "He will not be disheartened or crushed until he has established justice in the earth."[31] God is neither a smoking flax nor a crushed reed! For the sake of both peoples who are scripturally called Zion, he will not rest until their "righteousness goes forth as brightness, and [their] salvation as a lamp that burns."[32] God will yet have his torch in the earth. His human menorah will shine forth the light of his truth from enlightened individuals, from Israel, and from the church.

Ultimately, God will send the Messiah and effect the resurrection of the dead. At that time "those who have insight will shine brightly like the brightness of the expanse of heaven, and those who lead the many to righteousness, like the stars forever and ever."[33] God's lamp will fully become man's light.

[1] John 8:12.
[2] Luke 2:30-32.
[3] John 9:5.
[4] Matthew 5:14.
[5] John 14:12.
[6] Ephesians 5:8-10, New International Version.

[7] 1 Peter 2:9, New Revised Standard Version.

[8] Psalm 48:2.

[9] Psalm 122:3-4.

[10] L. Yarden, *The Tree of Light* (Ithaca, New York: Cornell University Press, 1971), p. 36.

[11] Psalm 48:2.

[12] Psalm 76:2.

[13] Deuteronomy 16:2; 2 Chronicles 6:20.

[14] Isaiah 2:3.

[15] Deuteronomy 16:16.

[16] Hebrews 12:22-23.

[17] Galatians 4:26.

[18] Acts 1:8.

[19] Luke 3:16.

[20] Acts 2:1-6.

[21] Acts 1:8.

[22] John 1:29, 36.

[23] Matthew 3:17.

[24] 2 Corinthians 4:6.

[25] Acts 10:1-31.

[26] Acts 13:47, New Revised Standard Version.

[27] Romans 11:29, New International Version.

[28] Isaiah 42:3-4, New American Standard Version.

[29] Carol L. Meyers, *The Tabernacle Menorah* (Missoula, Montana: Scholars Press, 1976), p. 20.

[30] Jeremiah 18:4, New Revised Standard Version.

[31] Isaiah 42:4, New American Standard Version.

[32] Isaiah 62:1, New King James Version.

[33] Daniel 12:3, New American Standard Version.

Chapter 11

The Tree
of Life

The similarity in appearance between the menorah and
a tree is neither coincidental nor the product of artistic li-
cense. The shape of the menorah with branches foliating
from its central stem is clearly patterned after a tree. The
Jewish people have long believed that the menorah originally represented the tree of life. The lampstand is clearly
a symbol of God's Word which David called "a lamp unto
my feet."[1] The tree of life is also identified with the Torah,
the wisdom of God's Word. Solomon declared that wisdom is a "tree of life."[2] In the Apocalypse, God says that
they "who do his commandments [Torah]" have a right "to
the tree of life."[3] Even without its flames of fire, then, the
menorah "contains supreme meaning, a message of God's
life-giving force and of the divine foundation of all existence."[4] Whether sustaining life in this world or securing
life in the world to come, the menorah as an iconographic
tree of life was crucial in the cultural milieu from which
Israel emerged.[5]

From the most ancient times, the arborescent symbol
representative of life's emerging from light has been a dominant literary and theological theme. In the beginning of creation, Adam and Eve were said to have had God's
permission to eat of the tree of life in the midst of the gar-

den;[6] however, they chose not to exercise their right of access to that tree, sampling instead the tree of the knowledge of good and evil.[7] As a consequence of violating the divine command, Adam and Eve were expelled from the garden. Their banishment was not, however, an act of divine retribution, but a manifestation of God's grace that made it impossible for them to "eat of the tree of life" and live forever in an irreconcilable state of sin. God's grace kept the progenitors of the human race and all their subsequent offspring from being eternal sinners, like the immortal fallen angels who have been reserved in chains of darkness forever since the moment of their rebellion against God.[8] Cherubim with flaming swords were stationed at the garden entrance to guard the way to the tree of life and to ensure the fact that mankind would not partake of it and become eternally unredeemable sinners.

It was only natural, then, that Adam and Eve and their descendants remember and perpetuate the understanding of the tree of life and the angels of fire. In the post-Edenic diaspora, many traditions emerged in various cultures concerning the tree of life. Inscriptions representing the tree of life as a seven-branched arborescent symbol have been discovered that may well predate the time of Abraham. Not only among the Jewish people, but also among many other cultures, the tree of life and the fire of the Divine have been dominant and connected themes.

The blending of tree and fire motifs is clearly seen in the profound incident of the burning bush that initiated the process which established the chosen people. Moses was called and commissioned by God himself in divine words spoken from a bush that was burning but not consumed.[9] Perhaps this was a preliminary manifestation of the menorah's rich symbolism to the prophet who would liberate Israel. God who "dwelt in the bush,"[10] was first manifest to Moses through this flaming bush. From the fire of the *Shekhinah* came the Word of God. The menorah likewise appears as a golden tree from which the fire is manifest that brings both light and life through God's Word.

The menorah also speaks of eternal life through the resurrection. Its arborescent symbolism, along with the mechanics of its operation, leaves this clear picture. In compliance with divine law, the pure oil used for the menorah light was exclusively from the olive tree. The ancients considered the olive tree to be eternal, a tree that never died; therefore, they regarded the olive tree as a symbol of enduring life.[11] An olive leaf was the first thing mentioned in Scripture as having survived the universal deluge in Noah's day,[12] bringing light to the world.[13] Olive trees presently exist that are more than 2,000 years old in the Garden of Gethsemane on the Mount of Olives. Even when the trunk of an olive tree is cut down, new life springs forth from its roots in the form of a *netzer*, a shoot.

This is, no doubt, what Job observed: "For there is hope for a tree, when it is cut down, that it will sprout again, and its shoots will not fail. . . . At the scent of water it will flourish and put forth sprigs like a plant."[14] In what is likely the oldest of biblical texts, Job used the imagery of the [olive] tree to express his personal hope of the resurrection: "If a man dies, will he live again? All the days of my struggle I will wait until my change comes. You will call, and I will answer you. . . . As for me, I know that my Redeemer lives, and at the last he will take his stand on the earth. And after my skin is destroyed, this I know, That in my flesh I shall see God."[15] From the most ancient of times, then, there is no doubt that the people regarded the olive

This Mesopotamian symbol from 3,000 B.C.E. is demonstrates the ancient tree design that was later manifest in the biblical menorah.

tree as a symbol both of enduring life and of the certainty of resurrection from the dead.

It is fitting, therefore, that the Jewish people have blended the imagery of the tree of life into the menorah as a symbol of after-life.[16] The idea of resurrection to a life of complete happiness on earth after the appearance of the Messiah and the establishment of the Golden Age is a specifically Jewish concept, unshared by any other ancient people. The Talmud describes this Jewish idea: "Not like this world is the world to come. In the world to come there is neither eating or drinking, no begetting of children, nor business transactions, no envy or hatred or rivalry; but the righteous sit enthroned with crowns on their heads, enjoying the brilliance of the Divine Presence."[17]

Because it was birthed from the matrix of Judaism, Christianity also makes faith in the coming of the Messiah and in the resurrection of the dead a part of its creed. John's words are distinctly parallel with those of the sages: "And I saw thrones . . . and they lived and reigned with Christ for a thousand years. . . The city had no need of the sun . . . for the glory of God illuminated it, and the Lamb is its light."[18] Jesus' comment about the age to come is equally parallel: "In the resurrection they neither marry, nor are given in marriage."[19]

It is no coincidence that much of the imagery employed in the menorah's design is also connected with the almond tree, the first tree in Israel to bloom when in mid-winter (occasionally as early as December, but usually in January or February) it decks itself in radiant white. Because of its appearance, the almond tree was thought of as a tree of light, traceable in tradition to the Edenic tree of life. The almond tree's earliest biblical name was *luz*, the name of the city that Jacob renamed *Beth-el* (God's house).[20] This etymological connection established a link between the almond tree and God's house that was visited by light-bearing angels.

In one wilderness incident, the almond rods that Moses had given to the leaders of Israel's twelve tribes were used to dig a well of water to sustain Israel.[21] The demonstration that the water of life was manifest through the agency of the almond tree has rich symbolism. The very survival of the thirsty Israelites was predicated on what must have appeared ridiculous, twelve leaders digging a well with almond rods. In connection with this symbolic act, it is also noteworthy that true biblical authority (signified by the twelve tribal leaders of Israel) is manifest in the act of bringing forth of life (the water of the Holy Spirit). Leadership among God's people is not merely positional and hierarchical, it is functional and facilitating, always bringing refreshment and life to thirsty souls.

The flowers on the branches of the menorah were almond flowers. Perhaps this motif is connected with the miraculous budding of Aaron's almond rod when the question of divine right to priesthood arose in the camp of Israel.[22] The desiccated, lifeless rod produced new life, manifesting a clear symbol of resurrection. When the dead rod budded, it confirmed Aaron's priesthood as the divinely commissioned channel for access to God. Apparent also is the messianic imagery of a Priest like Melchizedek who would be resurrected from the dead to be the light of life. Medieval Christian literature suggested that the cross of Christ,[23] as well as the "shoot from the stump of Jesse"[24] was prefigured in Aaron's rod. When Jesus resurrected from the dead, proof positive was offered that he was the High

Priest who was to bring the light of life to all men.[25] The menorah as the tree of life likewise symbolically brings life through the light of its lamps. Some have suggested that the Christmas tree with its lights shared the imagery both of the tree of life and of the menorah.[26] Though it has been suggested that this image was introduced by Martin Luther, it was likely an adaptation of pre-Christian ritual designed to lend light to the dying sun to replenish it for spring fertility.

The Hebrew word for almond, *shaked,* is from the root *shakod*, which also means "watching." The connection between the almond motif and the divine protection upon God's people is set forth by Jeremiah. Having seen "a rod of an almond tree [*shaked*]" in a vision, the prophet was assured by the Eternal: "I am watching [*shakod*] to see that my word is fulfilled."[27] The juxtaposition of the words *shaked* and *shakod* (*almond* and *watching*) makes an emphatic statement in the Hebrew of this text. Because the menorah is intrinsically tied with the almond tree, Israel's earliest blooming tree, it is a symbol of God's vigilance to provide eternal light for his people as well as an indication of Israel's prevailing before God with unceasing prayer.[28] The menorah is also a symbol of God's vigilance to overshadow his people, to watch over them with unceasing grace. "He who watches over Israel will neither slumber nor sleep."[29] The fact that the menorah was richly embellished with the almond motif reinforced the concept that the light of God's Word's is a tree of life to his people. The fact that it demonstrated the fiery light of God's truth manifest upon and within a tree is an unmistakable image of the light of life.

Among the Jewish people Torah scrolls (the Hebrew parchments of the Pentateuch) are wound on wooden dowels (usually olive wood) that are called *etz hayyim* (tree of life). The Torah is the record of God's instructions that, when fulfilled in men's lives, produce life. When asked what one should do "to inherit eternal life," Jesus himself responded: "Keep the commandments."[30] Walking in rebellion against the commandments of God that were explicitly set forth in the Torah tends toward darkness and death. Walking in faithfulness to the instruction that is estab-

The moriah plant, common to Israel, has striking similarities to the menorah.

lished in the Torah is an exercise in the light of life. "The law of the wise is a fountain of life," Solomon observed.[31]

The menorah is also said also to reflect the shape of the moriah plant in Israel, which until recently was plentiful on Mount Moriah, the ancient site of the *Akedah*, Abraham's binding of Isaac, and of the temples of Solomon and Zerubbabel. An Aramaic translation renders "Moriah" as "ritual," perhaps referring to the ritual of burning fragrant substances on the incense altar.[32] The moriah plant naturally releases its fragrance in the heat of the day when the sun reaches its zenith and radiates the most intense light of the day.[33] Light and fragrance were also brought together in the holy place of the Israelite sanctuary where the menorah's light was joined with the aroma of burning incense. It is not surprising that God connects light and fragrance in his instructions to Moses and Israel in Exodus 25:2, 6: ". . . bring me an offering . . . oil for the light, spices for anointing oil, and sweet incense. . ." The light of God's Word is sweeter than honey,[34] a truth confirmed by Solomon confirmed when he said, "Truly the light is sweet."[35]

The menorah is a symbol of arborescent Israel, the nation that has been God's family tree of salvation and covenant relationship since they were summoned to Sinai to receive his Word. Paul used the metaphor of the productive olive tree to describe ancient Israel.[36] Joel likened Israel to the fig tree.[37] It is fitting, therefore, that the menorah, *qua* tree of life, has historically been the most prominent symbol of the Jewish people as a nation. Though the Star of David has been popular in the past two centuries, the menorah has remained the material emblem *par excellence* for the Jewish people. Even the restoration of the Jewish state, the nation of Israel, was thought of in terms of resurrection. Theodor Herzl, the father of modern Israel, combined the images of menorah and tree when he wondered prophetically, "Would it not be possible to give back . . . to the menorah its life, to water its roots like those of a tree?"[38]

The menorah is also a symbol of the arborescent Messiah, the long-expected ruler in Israel who issues from the stem of Jesse (Isaiah 11:1) to become the Branch of the Lord (Zechariah 3:8). It has been suggested that the earliest believers in Jesus as Messiah were styled "*Notzrim*" because they were followers of the one whom they recognized as the *Netzer*, the branch from the root of Jesse,[39] the live shoot from the green olive tree,[40] the stock of Israel. It is quite appropriate, therefore, that the glorified Jesus was seen by the Revelator as standing in the midst of the menorah (seven golden lampstands). The Messiah is the Tree of Life, and the life that is inherent in his being is the light of men.[41] Both Jews and Christians believe that in the age to come, natural light will not be necessary, for God and/or the Messiah will be the light of God's people.[42]

Even without its lamps of fire, then, the menorah *per se* is filled with rich significance, demonstrating the tree of life manifest in the Garden of Eden, but now revealed in the light of the world, God's Word. It is of no small consequence that such an object, representing the tree of life that was first in Eden and in the Bible's final chapter finally appearing in heaven, was placed in Israel's tent of meeting and in all subsequent sanctuaries. "The tree of perception and realization of goodness and truth is a golden tree, made of gold from its roots to its flowers . . . pure and genuine in its every particle . . . representing utmost perfection."[43] The menorah, consummate in purity, perfect in design, made of pure gold demonstrates not a rigid form but a life of eternal, fruitful blossoming.[44] Only in the fiery light of God's Word can the tree of eternal life be found. Only in God's Lamp is man's light.

[1] Psalm 119:105.

[2] Proverbs 3:18.

[3] Revelation 22:14.

[4] Rudolph Brasch, *The Judaic Heritage* (New York: David McKay Co., 1969), p. 311.

[5] Carol L. Meyers, *The Tabernacle Menorah* (Missoula, Montana: Scholars Press, 1976), p. 180.

[6] Genesis 2:9.

[7] Genesis 3:6.

[8] Jude 6.

[9] Exodus 3:2.

[10] Deuteronomy 33:16.

[11] W. Wirgin, "The Menorah as Symbol of Judaism," *Israel Exploration Journal*, 14, 1964, p. 141.

[12] Genesis 8:11.

[13] *Midrash Tanchuma, Tezave 5,1*, quoted in Nogah Hareuveni, *The Emblem of the State of Israel: Its Roots in the Nature and Heritage of Israel* (Kiryat Ono, Israel: Neot Kedumim, 1988), p. 7.

[14] Job 14:7, New American Standard Version, 1995 edition.

[15] Job 14:14-15; 19:25, New American Standard Version; 19:26, New King James Version.

[16] W. Wirgin, "The *Menorah* as Symbol of After-Life," *Israel Exploration Journal*, 14, 1964, p. 102.

[17] Babylonian Talmud, *Berakhot* 17a.

[18] Revelation 20:4; 21:23.

[19] Matthew 22:30.

[20] Genesis 28:19.

[21] Numbers 21:18.

[22] Numbers 17:6-8.

[23] E.S. Greenhill, "The Child in the Tree: A Study of the Cosmological Tree in Christian Tradition," *Traditio*, x (1964), pp. 323ff.

[24] Isaiah 11:1ff; Romans 15:12.

[25] Acts 17:31.

[26] L. Yarden, *The Tree of Light* (Ithaca, New York: Cornell University Press, 1971), p. 37.

[27] Jeremiah 1:11-12.

[28] 1 Thessalonians 5:17.

[29] Psalm 121:4., New International Version.

[30] Matthew 19:17.

[31] Proverbs 13:14.

[32] Nogah Hareuveni, *The Emblem of the State of Israel: Its Roots in the Nature and Heritage of Israel* (Kiryat Ono, Israel: Neot Kedumim, 1988), p. 12.

[33] *Ibid.*, p. 25.

[34] Revelation 10:9-10.

[35] Ecclesiastes 11:7.

[36] Romans 11:17-20.

[37] Joel 1:7.

[38] *Die Welt*, Dec. 31, 1897, quoted in L. Yarden, *The Tree of Light* (Ithaca, New York: Cornell University Press, 1971), p. 53.

[39] Isaiah 11:1, 10.

[40] Luke 23:31.

[41] John 1:4.

[42] Revelation 21:23.

[43] S. R. Hirsch, *Selected Writings*, pp. 209-235, quoted at the Website: *http://members.tripod.com/~TheHOPE/menorah2.htm, p. 1.*

[44] *Ibid.*

Chapter 12

A Messianic Portrait

Many scholars have considered the menorah to be a symbol of Messianic and eschatological significance.[1] "The symbol of light, enclosed in darkness, became the symbol of hope and took on a new iconographic meaning–that of one of the prominent symbols pointing toward the Messianic era."[2] Among the most ancient of Messianic prophecies is that of Balaam: "I see him, but not now; I behold him, but not near; a Star shall come out of Jacob; a Scepter shall rise out of Israel."[3] The Messiah was to have the radiance of a star, a symbol of illumination. In one of the last Messianic prophecies of the Hebrew Scriptures, the Messiah was also to be the "sun of righteousness."[4] When the prophets and seers of Israel visualized the Messiah, they could describe him only in terms of the greatest, most intense light they could imagine. The apostles likewise saw Jesus as the day star[5] and the bright morning star.[6]

The many and diverse "paintbrush Christs," the inspirations of various artists, most frequently make inaccurate depictions of Jesus. He is generally portrayed with Nordic features, but occasionally he is depicted with African or Oriental features. The truth is that Jesus was a Jew, born and reared in a Torah-observant Jewish family. He may well have been less than handsome, perhaps even disfigured as Isaiah's prophecy suggests.[7]

In essence, the menorah can be seen as an ideal representation of Jesus as Lord and Messiah. The *Logos* has historically been understood as an eternal light surrounding God's throne. Is it any wonder, then, that when John viewed Jesus in his resurrected glory, he saw him in the midst of seven golden lampstands?[8] John had been Jesus' most intimate confidant, "the disciple whom Jesus loved."[9] At the beginning of his Patmos experience, however, he could only describe his Lord as "one like the Son of man" when he came face to face with the Son of God in his glory. The radiance of Jesus' countenance was so intense that "his face shone as the sun."[10] The eternal light of the one whose essence is light so overwhelmed John that he fell as dead before the glorified Jesus.[11]

When John encountered Jesus, he first saw seven golden lampstands, in the midst of which then he saw "one like the Son of man," a spectacular figure with eyes like flames of fire. Just as it had been in the Genesis account of the beginning of creation, a word issued forth producing the light from which God himself was revealed. John first heard God's voice, then he saw the menorah, then he recognized the Messiah, the Son of God. Whenever the Messiah is seen, he is manifest in light, the light that the menorah radiates.

The Messiah is the light who enlightens every man. Paul succinctly encapsulated this truth: "For God, who commanded the light to shine out of darkness, hath shined in our hearts, to give the light of the knowledge of the glory of God in the face of Jesus Christ."[12] On the Mount of Transfiguration, the inner circle of Jesus' disciples viewed their Messiah in his glory: "[Jesus] was transfigured before [Peter, James, and John]. His face shone like the sun, and his clothes became as white as the light . . . whiter than anyone in the world could bleach them."[13] The disciples saw Moses and Elijah and heard God's voice from the enshrouding cloud affirm Jesus' divine patrimony.[14]

With this fundamental understanding in mind, the introduction to the Apostle John's gospel takes on new significance: "In the beginning was the Word and the Word was with God and the Word was God. . . . In him was life, and the life was the light of men."[15] Jesus is the Torah incarnate, from whom sprang the primordial light that was manifest when God first spoke his Word. As John observed, Jesus was the *Logos* of God by whom all things were created, including the light. It is equally simple to recognize that the life that was (and is) manifest in the person of the Word is the light of men. John further teaches this light brings fellowship and atonement for sin.[16]

Many people conceive of the universe as a closed system that God summoned into being and then abandoned to its own eternally repeated order. The truth is, however, that God continually speaks the creative word, "Let there be light." His Word is the means by which the universe is sustained, for Jesus upholds *"all things by [his] word."*[17] If for one moment God should cease declaring, "Let there be light," total darkness would permeate the entire universe. If God's Word were to cease summoning forth the creation, the universe would collapse upon itself in a complete and utter implosion and terminate in nonexistence. Indeed, the *aleph* and the *tau* of existence were created simultaneously.

The creative and sustaining power of God's Word is a manifestation of his eternity, his absolute lack of beginning or ending. The Almighty is not limited by time or space. He lives in the eternal present, with no boundaries of past or future. Time is merely a function of mankind's finite intelligence, a part of the tri-universe that is wholly composed of time, space, and energy (including matter). Like its Creator, the universe is not part time, part space, and part energy: it is all time, all space, and all energy. God, however, is larger than the universe. For God, all of time co-exists simultaneously in the Alpha/Omega. With him, there is no dichotomy between past and future, for both are an eternal "now."

Even the Ineffable Name of God, Y/H/W/H, reveals God's eternity. "I am that I am," God responded when Moses inquired of his name. Likewise, Jesus declared, "Before Abraham was I am,"[18] not, "Before Abraham was I was." The God who created is the God who sustains because for him creation is the present and continuing act of the spoken Word.

The fact that the Word of God and light are synonymous is confirmed from nature. Both sound and light are of essentially the same energy. It is no coincidence that many physicists now believe that all of matter was created from sound waves. This idea is part of the string theory that seeks to unite the theories of relativity and quantum mechanics into one overarching law. Apparently the sound of God's Word that created light, the stuff of the universe, was the very substance of energy/matter. The instant that God separated from himself the essence that John called the *Logos*, the creative process was set into motion in a dynamic that continues to the present time and will continue forever. The light of God is manifest from the life that is in the written, spoken, and living Word.

THE MESSIAH AND THE ETERNAL LAMP

For generations before the time of Jesus, according to tradition, the central lamp of the menorah had burned miraculously throughout the day and night on the same amount of oil that the other six lamps needed to burn through the night. It was toward this central lamp that the wicks of the other six lamps were directed. Because of the continual burning of this lamp, it came to be called the *ner tamid*, the eternal light. It also came to symbolize God's eternal presence with Israel as guardian and protector.

Perpetually burning lamps in Jewish synagogues to this day recall this temple miracle and its significance to the Israelites. So important is the iconographic significance of the *ner tamid* that when a new synagogue is built, its eternal lamp is generally lit from the fire of a previously existing synagogue. Many Christian congregations also maintain an eternal light in their sanctuaries in a practice borrowed from Judaism (though many likely are not aware of this historical connection).

It is no coincidence that exactly forty years before the destruction of the temple, the *ner tamid*, the lamp on the central shaft of the menorah, was found to have gone out for the first time in generations. The sages observed that the extinguishing of the *ner tamid* coincided with the death of Simon the Just, the notable high priest and the last of the men of the Great Synagogue, exactly forty years before Titus destroyed the temple in 70 C.E.[19] This was also the time when Jesus was crucified. Was the extinguishing of the *ner tamid* God's way of graphically demonstrating to Israel that light of the Living Menorah had been snuffed out? This event signaled the beginning of a forty-year probationary time that preceded God's judgment upon the sanctuary and its cultus.

Coincidentally, the sages have also noted that at this same time, forty years before the temple's destruction, the scarlet thread that was tied between the horns of the scapegoat when the sins of Israel were confessed annually by the high priest was found not to have become white, as it had for generations. Was this God's sign to Israel that the sacrifices of animals were no longer efficacious? The one eternal sacrifice for sin had been made in the body that God had prepared for Jesus.[20] Both the extinguishing of the *ner tamid* and the scapegoat's unbleached cord were considered grave omens among the Jews of the time. Most of Israel's leaders, however, were not aware of the hour of their visitation.[21] The Messiah had come as God's light and as his salvation,[22] fully manifesting the menorah's eternal light and the eternal sacrifice that turns scarlet sins as white as snow.[23]

In reality, the *ner tamid* had been transferred from the temple menorah to the Living Menorah, the light incarnate. The transcendent essence of the Eternal God could not have been known except through the revelation of his Son: "Long ago God spoke to our ancestors in many and various ways by the prophets, but in these last days he has spoken to us by his Son, whom he appointed heir of all things, through whom he also created the worlds. He is the reflection of God's glory and the exact imprint of God's very being, and he sustains all things by his powerful word."[24]

Jesus uniquely and completely fulfilled the prophecy that had been directed to the nation of Israel, proclaiming them to be God's light to the nations: "I will also give you as a light to the Gentiles, that you should be my salvation to the ends of the earth."[25] Jesus fulfilled what Israel had been commissioned to do and had failed to accomplish. Through him, "the people who were sitting in darkness saw a great light, and those who were sitting in the land and shadow of death, upon them a light dawned."[26]

Through Jesus' disciples and those after them, the good news of God's dominion was heralded among all the world's nations for the obedience of faith.[27] As he had promised, Jesus, the light of the world, was with his disciples always, even to the end of the age,[28] illuminating their lives with his glory so that they became the light of the world and brought the light of God's salvation to the nations. No one can dispute the fact that untold myriads of believers among all the nations of the world for the past two millennia have received Israel's light, the eternal Word of God, through the agency of Christian believers, the body of Christ, commissioned and sent forth by Jesus himself.

The Jewish people have long believed that the primordial light that was manifest in the creation of the universe is the Royal Messiah. The church believes that Jesus was the light of the world before all creation, that he was the light of the world in his incarnation, and that he will be the only light in the age to come. John graphically demonstrated this truth in his vision of the holy city that he said would descend from heaven to earth.[29] After recounting the profound dimensions and glorious appointments of this city, he declared that it would have no need for sun or moon to enlighten its inhabitants, for "the Lamb is the light thereof."[30] The Lamb of God who removed the world's sin will forever be the world's light, even in the renovated heaven and earth.

According to Daniel's prophecy, the Royal Messiah would be one whose eyes would be as "lamps of fire."[31] John saw this Messiah as Jesus in the midst of seven golden lampstands[32] and later as the Lamb with "seven horns and seven eyes."[33] Zechariah also envisioned this same Messianic character who would be manifest as both priest and king,[34] bringing together into one both the civil and the spiritual authority. It is no coincidence that this same motif is repeated in Zechariah's vision of the menorah flanked by two olive trees.[35] The menorah is said to represent the "Lord of the whole earth." The two olive trees are the two offices of the Messiah, king and priest, represented contemporaneous to Zechariah's vision by Zerubbabel (the civil governor) and Joshua (the high priest).

The Messiah is the Person who was a stone with "seven eyes."[36] The seven lamps of fire manifest in the menorah, then, are emblematic of the eyes of the Messiah, the Stone that the builders rejected who became the chief cornerstone of the spiritual temple.[37] The seven eyes represent the seven channels of life and light that proceed from the Messiah through the agency of the Holy Spirit. These are manifest in the "seven spirits of God," the seven lamps of fire burning before God's throne.

The menorah, then, is a perfect iconographic portrait of the Messiah, both in the Hebrew Scriptures and in the Apostolic Writings. He was the divine light in the beginning of time. He was the source of illumination for the patriarchs and for the nation of Israel. He has been the light of life to all who have believed upon him since his ascension into glory. And he will be the eternal light of the universe in the endless ages of the world to come. He is uniquely the Living Menorah, the one who brings the pure, pristine light of the *Shekhinah*, the Eternal Presence, into the hearts of all those who will but accept his love. Jesus is God's Lamp and man's light.

[1] Roth, "Messianic Symbols in Palestinian Archaeology," *Palestine Exploration Quarterly* 87 (1955), p. 151-154.

[2] Daniel Sperber, "History of the Menorah," *Journal of Jewish Studies* XVI, 3, 4, p. 155.

[3] Numbers 24:17, New Kings James Version.

[4] Malachi 4:2.

[5] 2 Peter 1:19.

[6] Revelation 22:16.

[7] Isaiah 52:14.

[8] Revelation 1:12-13.

[9] John 21:20.

[10] Revelation 1:16.

[11] Revelation 1:17.

[12] 2 Corinthians 4:6, King James Version.

[13] Matthew 17:2, New King James Version; Mark 9:2, New International Version.

[14] Mark 9:7.

[15] John 1:1, 4.

[16] 1 John 1:7.

[17] Hebrews 1:3.

[18] John 8:58.

[19] Babylonian Talmud, *Yoma* 39b.

[20] Hebrews 10:5.

[21] Luke 19:44.

[22] Psalm 27:1; Isaiah 49:6.

[23] Isaiah 1:18.

[24] Hebrews 1:1-3, New Revised Standard Version.

[25] Isaiah 49:6, New Kings James Version.

[26] Matthew 4:16, New American Standard Version.

[27] Romans 16:26.

[28] Matthew 28:20.

[29] Revelation 21:10.

[30] Revelation 21:23, King James Version.

[31] Daniel 10:6.

[32] Revelation 1:12-13.

[33] Revelation 5:6.

[34] Zechariah 6:13.

[35] See Zechariah 4.

[36] Zechariah 4:9-10.

[37] Matthew 21:42.

Chapter 13

Menorah
Mystery Numbers

The construction of the menorah was to be according to the heavenly pattern, a fact that underscores the importance of the significant numbers that were employed in its design. Many mysteries of the Holy Scriptures are concealed and revealed through numbers. This is true of the menorah and the various numbers in its construction, each of which helps us understand more about God's system and the light that it brings to man.

ONE

In Hebrew, the center lamp of the menorah is called *ner Elohim* (the lamp of God). Both the central shaft and the center lamp are symbolic of God himself. Indeed, the middle lampstand itself is called the menorah in the blueprint of Scripture, with the other six branches identified as "his" (the middle lampstand's) branches. According to tradition, the lamps atop the other six branches were turned so that they faced the center. This is an indication that all light–indeed, everything–bows before and owes its existence as well as any luminescence it manifests to the One who inherently is Light.

The seven lamps of the menorah are styled "the seven spirits of God" in the Apocalypse. Since the Scriptures teach that God is love, the center lamp may well represent the spirit of love. Love is the bond of moral completeness;[1] therefore, it is the element that maintains the perfection symbolized by the seven lamps. This idea may well be supported by the fact that the central lamp is also called the *shamash*, or helper, in the sense that from this lamp the other lamps were lit each evening. This is a further indication that whatever light-bearing good works proceed from men's lives result from the fire of God's love that is kindled in their hearts by the Holy Spirit.

THREE

An analysis of the menorah's structure also manifests other biblical numbers that are significant to the believer. First, in the base of the menorah that was in the temple in 70 C.E., both the numbers *three* and *twelve* stand out. Rabbinic tradition and archaeology suggest that the menorah was supported by a tripod base. The number *three* represents the foundation of the Word of God, the *TaNaKh*–the *Torah* (Law), the *Nevi'im* (Prophets), and the *Ketuvim* (Hagiographa). Judaism also rests on a threefold foundation: Torah, temple, and chosen people.

Because Jesus maintained his identity with his own Jewish tradition, three witnesses were foundational to all of his teachings.[2] He always appealed to the Torah, the prophets, and the writings to confirm his teachings. The number *three* is also important to Christians who understand that the very foundation of all light is the one God of the Bible, who is manifest in three persons, Father, Son, and Holy Spirit.

SEVEN

The most obvious numerical device seen in the menorah is the number *seven*. There are seven lamps of fire atop the seven branches of the lampstand. The question that begs to be asked is, "Why seven?" The Jewish people have always seen in the menorah the number of perfection or completeness. "Only a life fully dedicated to God and suffused with spiritual light can reach perfection."[3]

The menorah has seven lamps to demonstrate the fact that the Holy Spirit is not restricted but encompasses a great diversity of elements. One lamp would have been sufficient to represent the Holy Spirit; however, seven were used to reveal the unity in diversity with which the Holy Spirit impacts the lives of men, enlightening them with spiritual perception and moral volition.

Seven in Holy Scripture is the number both of vision and of power. This is seen in the Lamb of God, who is described by John as "having seven horns and seven eyes, which are the seven spirits of God."[4] Horns are emblematic of power and authority while eyes are channels through which light is brought into the body. Zechariah describes these seven lamps of fire on the menorah as the "eyes of the Lord which run to and fro through the whole earth."[5] The number *seven*, then, manifests both power and illumination for vision.

As a power motif, seven is seen in the seven *shofarot* (ram's horns) that preceded the armies of Israel in their marches around the walls of Jericho, in the seven daily circuits and the seven circuits on the seventh day. It is also seen in the secret of Samson's phenomenal physical prowess, the *seven* locks of hair on his head. It is no coincidence that there are seven angels with seven *shofarot*, seven thunders, and seven bowls of wrath in John's apocalyptic vision.[6] These seven angels are equipped and authorized to manifest God's power that brings judgment on the earth in the time immediately preceding the Messianic Age.

The seven spirits are also connected with the seven angels in the Apocalypse. This follows from David's assertion that God "makes his angels spirits, his ministers a flame of fire."[7] The seven angels are the seven spirits, the seven flames before the throne of God. The letters from the seven angels (spirits) to the seven churches were visions from the fire of insight and illumination.

Both the Apocalypse and the book of Isaiah tell us that there are seven spirits of God. Isaiah lists them: the spirit of the Lord, the spirit of wisdom, the spirit of understanding, the spirit of counsel, the spirit of might, the spirit of knowledge, and the spirit of the fear of the Lord.[8] In the Apocalypse, John served as an amanuensis from these seven spirits to convey personal messages to the seven churches in Asia Minor. The concerns of these spirits in each of the churches help reveal their nature and function in much the same way as craftsmen of different disciplines can be identified by the construction flaws with which they are concerned. There are certainly parallels between the messages to the seven churches and the seven spirits listed in Isaiah.

In Israel's conquest of the Promised Land, seven priests led the way before the ark of the covenant, blowing *shofarot* announcing the fulfillment of God's promise to Moses. The same occurred in the New Testament church when seven men were chosen to administer the church's practical affairs. These were far more than "deacons" in the general sense of the word, for they included such powerful preachers of the Word as Philip, who was called "the evangelist,"[9] and Stephen, whose profound apology so impacted the leaders of Israel that he became the church's first martyr. Seven men were likely chosen to perpetuate the scriptural prominence of the number seven, perhaps even to connect with the seven Spirits of God. That the seven lamps of the menorah were to fulfill a foundational role in the church is clear in Scripture. Solomon declared that "wisdom has built her house, she has hewn out her seven pillars . . ."[10] It is no coincidence that the spiritual house of God, the church, rested on twelve foundational pillars (apostles)[11] and seven pillars of wisdom.[12]

In reality, there is only one Spirit of God, just as there is only one Lord, one faith, and one baptism; however, that one Spirit of God operates in relationship to the universe and especially to mankind through seven channels. It is these seven channels that bring vision and insight to the people of God. It is also these operations that manifest the power of God for the supernatural in the lives of believers.

Just as there is "one Spirit" that is revealed in seven channels, so there is "one baptism" that is manifest in seven baptisms that function in continuity with Judaism's principle of ritual immersion. A significant part of Jewish ritual involved "various baptisms,"[13] ceremonial ablutions that featured immersion in a *mikveh*, a pool of living water, filled from a running stream or from rain. When using the *mikveh* for ritual immersion, the worshiper would descend seven steps on one side, immerse himself, and ascend seven steps on the other side. This action came to symbolize a rebirth and a change of legal status. Such was the case when a proselyte to Judaism immersed himself in the *mikveh*. The moment he ascended from the water, he was no longer a Gentile, but a Jew.

The *mikveh* tradition was perpetuated in Christian faith. Judaism's "various baptisms" were perpetuated in immersions that were manifest first in the baptism of John and then in Christian baptism. Later as early believers in Messiah came to understand more clearly the spiritual experiences which they received through faith in Jesus, they used immersion as a principle to describe their experiences. John taught not only a baptism in water, but also a spiritual experience of the baptism of repentance.[14] Then, Paul emphasized baptism as parallel with circumcision, a process of sanctification.[15] As John the Baptizer had predicted, Jesus immersed his disciples in the Holy Spirit on the day of Pentecost.[16] John also spoke of baptism in fire, which is clearly parallel with and a part of baptism in the Holy Spirit.[17] Then, Jesus spoke of an immersion in suffering[18] and a final immersion, the experience of death,[19] which features a perfect *mikveh* manifestation of descending in death only to ascend in resurrection. In reality, all of seven baptisms form one immersion continuum which begins with initiation into faith and concludes in resurrection.

The Jewish people have always seen in the menorah the number of perfection or completeness. The six branches extending from the shaft of the menorah are emblematic of the six days of creation, while the central shaft and its perpetual light symbolize the Sabbath. Everything stems from the Creator; therefore, say the Jews, value is imparted to men's days from God's day of refreshment, *Shabbat* (the Sabbath). Holiness and perfection are achieved, not from men's days of work, but from the spiritual light emanating from God.

In a similar manner, the church has no righteousness, no splendor, no illumination except that which it receives from its attachment to the "Stem of Jesse," the Messiah. The church is the light of the world only to the extent that it is connected with Jesus and is imbued with his life and anointing. The fruit of life and light is found in the branches only as they are connected to the vine.[20]

TWELVE

The number *twelve* is manifest in the menorah from the portrayal of its base on the Arch of Titus as a two-tiered hexagonal platform. This base displays a total of twelve surfaces on which various graphic images are inscribed; however, the signs of the twelve tribes of Israel may have originally appeared there. The number *twelve* is significant in that it is the foundational number for much of God's activity among men. Twelve patriarchs were the foundational pillars of the nation of Israel.[21] Likewise, twelve apostles were the foundation of the reformed congregation that is now called the church.[22] Twelve is also seen in judgment. Moses recognized twelve leaders of the twelve tribes of Israel by giving them rods inscribed with their tribal names to symbolize their authority.23 Interestingly enough, there were twelve men that God used to judge Israel between the time of Joshua and the monarchy.[24] It was with these rods that they dug the well that provided life-giving water for Israel.[25] Jesus promised his twelve apostles that they would judge the twelve tribes of Israel.[26]

SEVENTY

In the various decorative elements of the menorah's branches the number *70* (ten times seven) appears. There were three capitals, three bowls, and three flowers (nine in all) in each of the six semicircular branches (a total of 54). The central shaft had four capitals, bowls, and flowers (a total of 12). Added together, these total 66, the exact number of books in the Christian canon of the Holy Scripture. An additional capital was said to be under each of the extended branches of the menorah (a total of three). These, added to the 66, make a total of 69. One additional capital, called the Golden Seventh Socket in the Septuagint, was likely added to the shaft of the lampstand, making a total of 70. The number *70* is significant in that there were 70 elders who received the impartation of Moses' spirit by the laying on of hands.[27] Interestingly enough, after Jesus had commissioned the twelve apostles, he also sent out 70 evangelists (prophets) to prepare the way before him, heralding the breaking forth of the kingdom.[28]

A PATTERN OF NUMBERS

The menorah contains the pattern for leadership that was manifest first in ancient Israel and then in the church. Just as all of Israel rests on the foundation of the twelve patriarchs, the seventy elders, and the seven priests who carried the ark, all of Christianity has been built on twelve foundational apostles, seventy prophets who proclaimed the good news, and seven men of wisdom. Through the teaching and practice of these men, the entire world has been illuminated by the light of truth. Both Israel and the church, then, have been the light of the world–God's lamp, man's light.

[1] Colossians 3:14.

[2] Luke 24:44.

[3] Rudolph Brasch, *The Judaic Heritage: Its Teachings, Philosophy, and Symbols* (New York: David McKay Company, 1969), p. 312.

[4] Revelation 5:6.

[5] Zechariah 4:10.

[6] Revelation 8:2; 10:3; 15:7.

[7] Psalm 104:4.

[8] Isaiah 11:2.

[9] Acts 21:8.

[10] Proverbs 9:1, New American Standard Version.

[11] Ephesians 2:20.

[12] Acts 6:3.

[13] Hebrews 9:10, New Revised Standard Version.

[14] Mark 1:4.

[15] Colossians 2:11-12.

[16] Acts 1:5.

[17] Matthew 3:11.

[18] Mark 10:39.

[19] Matthew 20:23.

[20] John 15:1-5.

[21] Exodus 28:21; Revelation 21:12.

[22] Ephesians 2:20; Revelation 21:14.

[23] Numbers 17:2-6.

[24] Othniel, Ehud, Shamgar, Deborah, Gideon, Jotham, Tola, Jephthah, Ibzan, Elon, Abdon, and Samson.

[25] Numbers 21:18.

[26] Matthew 19:28.

[27] Numbers 11:16, 26.

[28] Luke 10:1. The *Textus Vaticanus* states that Jesus sent 72 evangelists, rather than 70 as other texts suggest. If this rendering is preferred, 72 parallels the 70 whom Moses anointed, plus the two (Eldad and Medad) who prophesied in the camp of Israel at the time when they were ordained.

Chapter 14

"By My Spirit," Says the Lord

The menorah is the centerpiece of one of the most powerful images in Bible prophecy. It is an extended metaphor that speaks powerfully to both Jew and Christian of the importance of manifesting the divine light through the Holy Spirit to accomplish God's purposes in the earth.

When a remnant of the Jewish people returned to Jerusalem following the Babylonian captivity, they discovered utter devastation, layered over with seventy years of accumulated debris and undergrowth. What had been an astonishingly beautiful city was hardly recognizable. The temple that had been among the world's most opulent architectural achievements lay in rubble. As they approached Mount Zion and surveyed the devastation, the tears that had flooded their parents and grandparents' eyes as they witnessed the destruction of their holy city and were led away in chains to Babylon now flowed from their own eyes.

How could such a feeble people, sorely lacking in resources and personnel, even contemplate rebuilding what elaborate planning, abundant capital, limitless artisans, and international cooperation had produced when Solomon had built the temple envisioned and planned by his father David? More than eighty percent of the Jewish population of Babylon, including the best minds, the most skilled craftsmen, and the strongest backs, had chosen to remain in that foreign land rather than return to Israel and face the hardships of rebuilding.

The task must have seemed daunting, even impossible. Though God had commissioned and inspired men of vision and passion to leave the comforts of Babylon to take on the challenge of restoring the holy city and its temple, there just were not enough of them. Because of their servitude in Babylon, they lacked funds to undertake such a massive task. They could well have shrugged their shoulders and acknowledged, "We cannot possibly do this work," and have simply walked away. Rather than wallow in despair, however, men like Nehemiah, Ezra, and Zerubbabel began to organize the personnel at their disposal and to set about systematically to accomplish the task of rebuilding. Their initial efforts, however, were so insignificant that they were mocked by their neighbors: "If a fox were to run on your wall, it would crumble!" they taunted these "feeble Jews."[1] Still, they kept plodding on, their goal ever before them.

These restorers knew who they were: "We are the servants of the God of heaven and earth,"[2] they declared. And they knew precisely what their mission was: "We are rebuilding the temple that was built many years ago, which a great king of Israel built and completed."[3] With such focus and passion, they continued over many arduous years the work of reconstruction. They built the walls of the city of Jerusalem with Nehemiah's simple strategy: each family worked on the portion of the city wall that was in front of its own house.[4] With great effort, they relaid the foundations of the temple and restored the altar so that the worship of the Eternal could be renewed in the place where he had commissioned it.

In the midst of all the frustration and turmoil, God himself spoke words of counsel and encouragement to the leaders of his people through those prophets of restoration who were among Israel's political and spiritual leaders. Haggai had issued God's command to his people: "Yet now take courage, O Zerubbabel, says the Lord; take courage, O Joshua, son of Jehozadak, the high priest; take courage, all you people of the land, says the Lord; work, for I am with you, says the Lord of hosts."[5] Though the temple they were building compared to Solomon's temple "as nothing," the prophet predicted, "The glory of this latter temple shall be greater than the former, says the Lord of hosts."[6]

Apparently in a time of great struggle a similar word came to Zechariah as an angel awakened him from sleep and presented a spectacular vision before his eyes. He saw a "lampstand of solid gold with a bowl on top of it, and on the stand seven lamps with seven pipes to the seven lamps. Two olive trees are by it, one at the right of the bowl and the other at its left."[7] When Zechariah was asked if he knew the import of the vision, he replied, "No, my Lord." The angel then declared that the vision was "the word of the Lord unto Zerubbabel," to be accompanied by this rubric: "Not by might, nor by power, but by my spirit, says the Lord of hosts."[8] Then the message continued to declare that the great "mountain" of opposition that was before the governor of Judea would be rolled flat into a plain. Finally, the comforting promise was made to Zerubbabel that his hands that had laid the foundation of the temple would finish it.

The message, "Not by might nor by power, but by my Spirit," is exactly seven words in the original Hebrew text: "לֹא בְחַיִל וְלֹא בְכֹחַ כִּי אִם־בְּרוּחִי (*lo b'chail v'lo b'khoach, ki im b'ruchi*)." Certain Jewish traditions suggest that Zechariah understood the import of the menorah vision when he saw these seven words in the flames above the seven lamps of the lampstand.[9] As the prophet saw these words, the message from the Divine to Zerubbabel was clear. It was the

The emblem of the Nation of Israel, featuring the elements of Zechariah's vision, the menorah and two olive branches.

same message that Israel had always heard from its prophets and sages: Light conquers might.

The connection between the illuminating menorah vision and the thunderous words, "Not by might, nor by power, but by my Spirit, says the Lord," could not, therefore, have been more lucid. From its beginning Israel's task had always been impossible. It had always a call, not to military might, but to faith in the miraculous power of God. It had been a commission that could be fulfilled only by divine enlightenment and empowerment, not by human strength and understanding. Ultimately, victory can never be established through conquest on the edge of the sword, and success can never be achieved through the actualization of human potential. Victory is achieved through enlightenment, and success is the result of divine empowerment. Israel's strength would always be divine light, not military might.

Zechariah's message to Israel was what should have been obvious to them, given their history and current situation. If they were to restore the temple and rebuild Jerusalem, it would only be through the empowerment of the Holy Spirit of the living God. With the agency of the *Shekhinah* (the localized fiery manifestation of the Holy Spirit), no mountain of opposition could stand before the people as they fulfilled God's will in the earth. They found that it is the menorah's light that crushes darkness, reducing the mountain of doubt and of human and demonic opposition to dust. They were like their ancestors in the wilderness who found that the *Shekhinah* that "came between the camp of the Egyptians and the camp of Israel . . . was a cloud and darkness to the one, and it gave light by night to the other."[10]

Interestingly enough, Zechariah's vision was further explained to the prophet. He was told that the two olive trees that he saw adjacent to the menorah were the two "shining ones" (anointed ones) that stand by the Lord of the whole earth. The menorah, then, was emblematic of God himself, the source of Israel's light and strength, and the lamps were symbols of his eyes. God is, indeed, light, of such intensity that he can be experienced only as that light is channeled through seven lamps, which John identified as the "seven spirits of God." When one "sees" God, he sees him only through the sevenfold light of his Spirit, which illuminates his Word, the fullest disclosure of his being that God has chosen to manifest.

The two shining ones to whom Zechariah referred were historically Zerubbabel and Joshua, the political and priestly leaders of Israel at the time. They were responsible for providing the resources necessary to make the menorah shine brightly to all of Israel. As the ancient Israelites were commissioned to provide pure olive oil to cause the light to shine, so these leaders were to provide purity of vision and purpose from the secular and religious dimensions so that the people could complete the task of restoration.

The Zechariah vision has remained a clear word for the Jewish people throughout their generations. They, above all peoples, understand that their survival and success are entirely dependent upon God's provision. Having endured innumerable onslaughts of discrimination, persecution, and violence, they exist as an identifiable people solely on the merit of their covenantal relationship with God. Defying all the laws of assimilation of conquered peoples, they have maintained their distinctive identity because God never changes[11] and because his gifts and callings are irrevocable.[12] Israel exists neither by might, nor by power, but by God's Spirit.

It is entirely appropriate, then, that the official emblem for the reborn nation of Israel displays the symbols of Zechariah's vision, the menorah and the olive branches. This emblem signifies for the Jewish people themselves and for the rest of the world that Israel is called to be the light of the world–both the menorah and the olive tree–bringing illumination and peace to all men of good will.

MYSTERIES FOR CHRISTIANS

Zechariah's vision also speaks to Christians around the world, particularly in the present era, which is arguably a prophetic time of restoration. Peter predicted that second advent of the Messiah would be such a time of restoration: "[God will] send the Messiah appointed for you, that is, Jesus, who must remain in heaven until the time of universal restoration that God announced long ago through his holy prophets."[13] The coming of the Messiah will feature the greatest restoration in the history of planet earth, as everything will be renewed and restored to the condition of the Garden of Eden. Before this great event, however, the world will witness an era of restoration, a preparation for the onset of the Messianic Age. If the church is presently in the time of the "birth pangs" of the Messianic Age (the term that many Jews use to describe their own Messianic expectations), then it is now a time of restoration.

There are close parallels between the spiritual work that God is doing among believers in this time and the natural accomplishments of the restorers in Zechariah's day. The history of the physical temple from the time of Solomon through the time of Zerubbabel allegorizes events in the history of the Christian church from the first century until the time of Jesus' second coming. This is in keeping with the apostolic hermeneutic that events under the first covenant foreshadowed events that were to occur under the new covenant.[14]

Just as Solomon's temple was destroyed and Israel was enslaved in Babylon, so the church which Jesus and the apostles built as a spiritual temple unto God experienced captivity in the same philosophy and religious ideas that were characteristic of ancient Babylon. The Jewish heritage of Christian faith was gradually replaced by the Hellenism of the Greco-Roman world as the church became increasingly Gentile both in leadership and in demographics. Just as Jerusalem was layered over with the rubble of conquest and the subsequent undergrowth of neglect, so the foundations of the earliest Jewish church were covered with accretions of human philosophy and pagan practices.

As the church began its expansion into the Greco-Roman world of the Mediterranean basin and beyond, accommodations were made with the dominant philosophies of the Hellenic world: neo-Platonism, Stocism, and even Gnosticism. Many of the prominent leaders of the church in the patristic period were neo-Platonist philosophers before their conversion to Christianity. They brought with them much of their tradition and philosophy which they sought to blend with the Hebraic teaching of Jesus and the apostles. Some even posited that the same God who spoke to Moses also spoke to Socrates, Plato, and Aristotle, and that Plato was a Christian even though he was unaware that he was!

As they approached the pagans of the Gentile kingdoms, the church's leaders tried to contextualize the Hebraic message of the gospel; however, they often crossed over the line into syncretism, consciously taking the religious ideas and practices of the nations they sought to convert and covering them with a thin veneer of "Christian" terminology and practice. Much of the pagan world continued to function as it had for centuries, with new names and new titles for the same deities and practices.

By the time of the Middle Ages, the church was hardly recognizable as a Hebraic entity, the ideal Jewish congregation that had been restored by Jesus and the apostles. It became thoroughly Gentile in mind-set and world view. The Platonizing of Christianity reduced it to a religion held captive in the stronghold of dualism, separating the secular and spiritual realms. Concepts and practices totally foreign to anything that Jesus and the apostles believed and taught became the dogma and polity of the medieval church. For all practical purposes, the church of Jesus, the temple of God, was in Babylonian captivity in ideas and practices that came from that ancient bastion of perverted humanist and polytheistic religion. Compared with what it was in the time of Jesus and the apostles, the church was desolate–its walls demolished, its foundations overturned, its facade covered with the undergrowth.

Enter this scene men and women of God who remembered the church's former glory and were impassioned with a vision to bring about restoration. At the beginning of the sixteenth century, there were calls both from within and outside the Western church for repentance, reformation, and renewal. Men who styled themselves "Christian Hebraists"[15] began to assert that in order to understand its mission and ministry the church should return solely to the Hebrew Scriptures (*sola scriptura*) rather than to historical ecclesiastical traditions. They also insisted that the church return from its sacramentalism and works-based righteousness to the Hebraic idea of justification solely through acceptance of God's loving kindness, i.e. "by grace through faith" (*sola fide*).

These reformers advocated "*Hebraica veritas*"[16] (Hebrew truth), insisting that the Scriptures could be rightly interpreted only with the grammatico-historical hermeneutic–that is, in the context of the grammar of Scripture[17] and of the culture and history of the Jewish people for whom and through whom the Bible was manifest. What was occurring, in effect, was a restoration of many of the foundations of the heavenly Jerusalem, the church. It was the beginning point for a long, arduous task that has encountered delays, detours, and reversals as centuries of time have unfolded; however, it is a task to which reformers and restorers of subsequent generations have devoted their energies and their lives, a passion to know God that could not and cannot be quenched. The radical reformation of restoration continues to expand, reaching every segment of the church and every nation of the world.

The sad truth is that fervor for restoration truth has often been swallowed up all too quickly in nationalism, denominationalism, separatism, and exclusivity. The entire church, Eastern and Western, Catholic and Protestant, still to this day maintains much non-biblical and occasionally outright anti-biblical teaching and practice. To the degree that this is true, the church walks in darkness, stumbling blindly along, injuring itself and society around it.

Unfortunately, now, as then, the fires of revival and restoration still too often burn brightly only to be reduced to embers and finally to ashes. Prophets of insight for restoration are replaced by bureaucrats who, rather than seeking fresh fire of insight from God, resort to memorializing the ashes of yesterday's fire, creating a crystallized system that precludes further progress in restoration. Like Abraham's family, these movements left Babylon bound for the Promised Land; however, they found themselves hung up in Haran. Still, God has always found someone who would hear the summons of his voice: "Get up and go." He will always raise up those who remember that the quest for restoration is accomplished not by might or power but by the sevenfold Spirit of God and by the illumination that the Eternal presence brings to those who pour the pure oil of the Holy Spirit into the menorah's waiting lamps.

This metaphor could not be more significant than at the present time, when preparation for the Messianic Age signals a time of restoration[18] very much parallel to what was occurring in Zechariah's day. Like Ezra, Nehemiah, Zerubbabel, Joshua, Haggai, and Zechariah, today's restorers are demanding the restoration of the ancient City of God, which a great King in Israel, Yeshua HaMashiach, established centuries ago.[19] No egomaniac jockeying for power, prestige, or perquisites here, no private agendas or personal kingdom-building, no dwelling in "paneled houses" while God's house lies waste![20] The identity of these people is in bond-slavery to God,[21] and their mission is simple: restoring the biblical congregation to become the city of God.

This restoration is encapsulated in the paradigm of the menorah. It is a work that even now is expanding exponentially as the Holy Spirit summons the church to restore the ancient paths wherein is the good way.[22] The menorah is a living emblem that demonstrates to the church and synagogue that the pure olive oil of the Holy Spirit will bring forth the light of eternity to guide people on this planet until the arrival of the Messiah.

LIGHT–A COLLABORATIVE EFFORT

Additional insights that can be gained from Zechariah's vision involve the two olive trees that were the source of the oil which caused the menorah to burn brightly. First and foremost, this vision is a messianic portrait, demonstrating the fact that the light of God shines most brightly when the God of the whole earth is manifest in his offices of priest and king. The two shining ones (anointed ones) are the two offices of the Messiah, who will be seen as both king and priest in his kingdom. This fact is further confirmed in Zechariah's vision of the man whose name is the BRANCH,[23] who sits enthroned as king and priest with a peaceable counsel between these two functions and parts of his nature. Jesus is the fulfillment of these prophecies, for he is the Branch of the Lord from the stem of Jesse[24] who is both king and priest.

Secondly, by interfacing Zechariah's vision with Paul's olive tree metaphor,[25] one can see that in the time for the ultimate manifestation of God's light, the two biblical nations that will provide pure oil for the light will be the Jews and the Gentiles. In the fullness of time both Jews and Gentiles will stand together supporting the light of the menorah, the fire of divine revelation for the entire world.

In this era of preparation for the Messianic Age, is it not time for both Jewish and Christian communities to rise up and relight the menorah, bringing forth the radiance of God's lamp to be man's light? In a time when iniquity abounds and the love of many has consequently grown cold,[26] both Israel and the church need to be blazing menorahs that illuminate the pathway to eternal life. While enemies of God mock both Jewish and Christian communities for their devotion to God and his Word, is it not time to realize that we can prepare for the coming Messiah only by working together to cause God's light to illuminate the world?

The ancient word of instruction from the Almighty still resounds to both Jews and Christians declaring the truth that the task of bringing the world from the doom of darkness into the light of hope is accomplished only by the Spirit of God. Could it be that the menorah will burn its brightest when God's two covenant peoples come alongside one another to share resources and insight for the quest of illuminating the world?

The message is as clear now as it was then: it is not by military might or by the power of men that ultimate victory is achieved. It uniquely results from the Holy Spirit's manifestation in the midst of God's people. It is the menorah's light that crushes darkness, reducing the mountain of doubt and of human and demonic opposition to the dust of a plain. God will always have anointed vessels, both Jews and Christians, through whom he will provide the pure beaten olive oil that makes the menorah burn brightly. It is by God's Spirit, not man's strength. It is God's lamp that brings man's light.

[1] Nehemiah 4:2, 3.

[2] Ezra 5:11a, New King James Version.

[3] Ezra 5:11b, New King James Version.

[4] Nehemiah 3:10.

[5] Haggai 2:4, New Revised Standard Version.

[6] Haggai 2:9, New King James Version.

[7] Zechariah 4:2-3, New King James Version.

[8] Zechariah 4:6, New King James Version.

[9] Nogah Hareuveni, *The Emblem of the State of Israel: Its Roots in the Nature and Heritage of Israel* (Kiryat Ono, Israel: Neot Kedumim, 1988), p. 8.

[10] Exodus 14:20, New King James Version.

[11] Malachi 3:6.

[12] Romans 11:29.

[13] Acts 3:20-21, New Revised Standard Version.

[14] Matthew 11:13; Colossians 2:17; Hebrews 10:1.

[15] Jerome Friedman, *The Most Ancient Testimony* (Athens, Ohio: Ohio University Press, 1983), p. 13.

[16] *Ibid.*

[17] The grammar of Scripture was originally Hebrew. Even the Apostolic Writings were first thought in Hebrew and then translated into Aramaic and Greek. Faithfulness to the grammatico-historical hermeneutic, therefore, demands understanding of the original language of Scripture, biblical Hebrew.

[18] Acts 3:20-21.

[19] Ezra 5:11.

[20] Haggai 1:4.

[21] Romans 1:1; James 1:1; 2 Peter 1:1; Jude 1; Revelation 1:1.

[22] Jeremiah 6:16.

[23] Zechariah 6:12.

[24] Isaiah 11:10; Romans 15:12.

[25] Romans 11:17-24.

[26] Matthew 24:12.

Chapter 15

Dedication Produces Light

One of the most poignant stories involving biblical symbols is the basis for Hanukkah, the Jewish festival that recalls the time in history when the Jewish people won a determined struggle for the heart and soul of Judaism and of all subsequent biblical religion. The central figure in this story is the menorah, the symbol of divine light. Because of the menorah's prominence, this Festival of the Dedication has also been called the Festival of Lights. Hanukkah celebrates the triumph of the menorah's light over Zeus' might.

In the era following the restoration of Jerusalem after Israel's Babylonian captivity, the Jewish people experienced a time of rapidly shifting political situations. Various kingdoms that surrounded the tiny province of Judea vied for military or political control over this key area. The land of promise had always been a place of conflict, for it formed the land bridge at the confluence of three continents, Europe, Asia, and Africa. As such, it was an invaluable passage both for trade and for the exercise of political power.

Alexander the Great had marched his armies virtually unopposed over the entire Middle East and had extended the Macedonian/Greek empire beyond into India. When he died, his empire was divided among his four generals, one of whom was Seleucus (*Seleukos* in Greek). The entire Middle East, then, came under the aegis of the Seleucid dynasty. From that time, conflict between the Ptolemys of Egypt and the Seleucids of Syria for control of Israel was continuous.

Immediately prior to the events that led to the celebration of Hanukkah, the Ptolemys had brought Judaea under their hegemony. Their rule was despised, as was all foreign imposition of authority and religious intimidation. During this time, Antiochus IV set out to expand the Seleucid empire and succeeded in expelling Ptolemy from Judaea. Initially, the leaders of Israel considered this an auspicious event, for Antiochus seemed to have come in peace and had freed them from Ptolemaic oppression.

After some three years of seeming benevolence in which he acted amicably toward Judea, Antiochus adopted a policy of forcing "civilization" on the various provinces under his power. He demanded that all his subjects accept the philosophy and religion of the Greeks. Initially, he promoted syncretism, a blending of the concepts of Hellenism with the religions and philosophies of the many "uncivilized" peoples in his realm. When such efforts confronted Israel, they were welcomed by much of the aristocracy of Jewish society which sought accommodation with the neighboring civil and religious powers in order to improve their political and economic positions.

This threat to Jews and Judaism was particularly insidious, for it was an attack at Judaism's very foundation–it's monotheism and its holistic world view. The attempted Hellenization of Judea, therefore, met with the strongest of opposition from those devoted to God and to the temple cult. Both Antiochus and his allies in Israelite society were openly rebuked for their affront to God and his Word. As resistance mounted, Antiochus determined to convert Israel to Hellenism on the edge of the sword, and a reign of terror ensued.

By this time, Antiochus, like so many pagan emperors of history, had come to view himself as divine, even

assuming the title *Epiphanes*, "God manifest." This Seleucid megalomaniac proceeded to demand that all Israel worship the Greek pantheon of gods or face torture and
execution. He brought into Yahweh's temple a statue of
Zeus, the king of the Greek gods, and inaugurated worship
to the idol image that involved sacrificing swine on the
temple altar. He also established houses of prostitution
within the temple confines, and he engaged in ritual murder of those who opposed his policy of forced Hellenization. The three commandments which Jews must not break
even at the expense of suffering martyrdom[1] were regu-
larly violated in the very temple itself.

Finally, in disgust and anger, certain Judeans cried out,
"Enough!" Led by Judas, the son of Mattathias, they
mounted a guerilla action against the Seleucid occupational
force. Because of his success, Judas was dubbed Macca-
bee (hammer). This campaign continued until Antiochus
and his forces were expelled from Judea. The Seleucid idola-
ter who had exalted himself not only against the Jewish people
but also against God himself was smitten with a disease so
horrible that his own physicians could not stand to attend him.
He died an agonizing death at Gabbae of Persis.

When the victorious Maccabees returned to the des-
ecrated temple, they found that most of its wealth and splendor had been plundered by the Seleucids. The pollution of the
holy things of the temple was disgusting, but it paled in com-
parison to the presence of idol images in the sanctuary. First
the Maccabees destroyed the idol images and their attendant
cultus. Then, they demolished the houses of prostitution that
had been erected in the temple complex. Finally, when all the
abominations had been removed, they set about to restore
temple worship to its former order and state.

Among the artifacts that had been plundered and destroyed by Antiochus was the temple menorah, most likely
the same one that had been fashioned by the exiles who

returned to Jerusalem after the Babylonian captivity. Aside from its obvious monetary value, Antiochus had destroyed the menorah as a symbolic gesture of his intention to extinguish the light of Judaism and replace it with Hellenism.[2] It was fitting, then, that after the heathen imposter and his pagan religion had been driven from the temple, the menorah, the symbol of Judaism's light, should be restored.

Since there was no candelabrum on which to ignite the sacred flame that symbolized the divine presence among God's people, the soldiers improvised a substitute. Taking seven of their hollowed spearheads, the very symbols and devices of their victory, they soldered them together with tin to form a makeshift menorah.[3] At that time, spearheads were hollow so that when armies were not engaged in battle they could be filled with oil and used as torches to light the way.[4] The Maccabean victors, therefore, poured oil into their spearheads, making lamps of the only lampstands available to them so that there might be a *ner tamid* in the temple. The symbolism of this menorah became more poignant and poetic: the very weapons of the war of liberation became the apparatus for raising the light.[5] The soldiers thereby also graphically signified that the Light of Israel, their God, not their physical weapons, had been the source of their victory and of the light of life and freedom that he had brought to them.

Because of the Jewish aversion to bringing weapons into the temple and of using iron in temple construction,[6] it is likely that they immediately began construction of a menorah of silver or other metal until a menorah of gold could be fabricated. When a search was made to find consecrated olive oil for lighting the menorah, one flask alone was found that had not been broken or pollutted, representing only a single day's supply.[7] Within little more than a month after the Maccabees entered the temple compound, the entire sanctuary had been cleansed, and its implements had been prepared for the resumption of temple worship.

The altar itself had to be purified seven days before public sacrifices could be offered.[8] Finally, on Kislev 25 in 165 B.C.E., the lamps were lit on the menorah.[9]

Tradition says that a miracle occurred when the lampstand was rekindled. The consecrated oil should have burned in the menorah for only 24 hours. Then the menorah could not have been lit for at least seven days, the time required to produce more consecrated oil. The flames, however, continued to rise from the lamp of God for an additional seven days. This was a witness to God's acceptance of his people's dedication and sacrifice both to achieve the victory over pagan forces and to restore his sanctuary to a state of ritual purity. It was a graphic demonstration to the Jewish people that God's approval was instant and evident upon their dedication.

The victory over Antiochus and the miracle of the light were causes for celebration among the Jewish people. Apparently the annual festival of Hanukkah was instituted immediately and became instantly popular. A century later, Mattathias Antigonos (40-37 B.C.E.), placed the image of the menorah on coins minted in his regime. The symbolism of the coins was obvious: in addition to proclaiming Mattathias as high priest of the temple cult, the coins' depiction of the menorah was a daily reminder to the Jewish people of their ancestors' exploits that had liberated them and had maintained the light of Judaism in their society.[10] Since that time, the Jewish people have celebrated the Festival of the Dedication to remember their victory over the syncretism with Hellenism that would have eviscerated Judaism. They have also rejoiced in the miracle of the light. Hanukkah joined the two seven-day Torah festivals, Unleavened Bread (called Passover) and Tabernacles, as the only week-long festivals in Judaism.

By the time of Jesus, the annual commemoration of Hanukkah was prominent among the Jews in Judea. Jesus himself was present for its celebration in Jerusalem,[11] indicating that he not only remembered the holy days required in the Torah but also participated in the post-Torah festivals as well. Indeed, the only biblical reference to Hanukkah is this notation of Jesus' presence at its celebration.

This is a clear indication that Jesus was altogether an observant Jew, fully a part of his community and national tradition. He was neither a renegade nor an innovator; he did not reject the tradition of his ancestors and contemporaries to initiate a new religion. Indeed, Jesus never changed his religion but sought to restore it to constitute "the ideal Israel."

Over time, the celebration of Hanukkah took the form of the lighting of one lamp of an eight-branched menorah for each of the festival's eight days. As successive days passed, another lamp was lit until all eight lamps burned on the eighth day. Because rabbinic tradition forbade the use of the lamps in kindling each other, a ninth branch was added to serve as a *shamash* (helper) lamp from which other lamps were lit in their proper order, Tradition also forbade all secular use of the Hanukkah menorah, including illumination for reading or working.[12] This, then, was the origin of the nine-branched menorah that is called the *hanukkiah* because of its use solely at the time of Hanukkah.

Today, Hanukkah is perhaps the second most popularly observed of the Jewish festivals (after Passover). It is important to Jews both for its imagery and for its memorialization of Judaism's victory over the intrusion of a pagan philosophy and religion into its ethical monotheism. It is also a celebration of freedom to worship the Creator according to his commandments. It is both a community, a family, and an individual event. The custom of many Jewish families is that each member of the family should light a Hanukkah menorah so that if there are five members in a family, there could be five lamps burning on the first day of Hanukkah, ten on the second day, and finally, forty for the eighth day, one light for each family member for each day of the festival. This underscores the fact that the responsibility for preserving freedom and letting the Torah's light shine is upon each individual, not just on the community and its leaders.

Each year, Jewish homes around the world are illuminated with the brightness of the *hanukkiah* as they celebrate victory over oppression and false religion, honor the maintenance of purity in celebration of the Torah against syncretism and compromise, and enjoy the blessing of light that is produced by dedication.

HANUKKAH LESSONS FOR CHRISTIANS

Christians could well profit from the festival of Hanukkah, especially when they recall that it was important enough for Jesus himself to be present in Jerusalem for its commemoration. There are clear lessons in this festival that will help Christian believers to come to greater maturity and aid in the fulfillment of their commission to be the light of the world.

Hanukkah teaches believers that dedication to God's ways always produces light. It was the act of rededication of the temple that set the stage for the miracle of light. The determination of the Jewish people not to be infected with pagan religion and philosophy enabled them to gain victory over Antiochus Epiphanes. The same determination prodded them to exercise extreme care so that the temple was cleansed, purified, and rededicated to God. When they completed this task and offered their results to God, he met with them with a confirming miraculous fire. They learned that even when men's resources are limited, the light of divine revelation and insight is boundless.

A clearer understanding of the dedication that produced the light is gained from an analysis of the Hebrew root word which is the source of the word *Hanukkah*. The word *hanakh* means "to initiate, to dedicate, to narrow, to educate." When one dedicates, he narrows the use of something, restricting it within specific parameters. He also initiates or begins a new or limited use.

The narrowing process underscores the words of Jesus in which he declared that both the way and the gate to everlasting life are narrow.[13] Indeed, the path to the hereafter is an ever-narrowing way. As the believer walks the road toward eternal life, he finds the way ever more constricted as God reveals more of his will and Word and expects obedience. This is the process of sanctification through the truth.[14] The manifestation of truth is the manifestation of light: "Send forth your light and your truth, let them guide me; let them bring me to your holy mountain, to the place where you dwell."[15] Could it be that the confining and ever-narrowing limits of this path where God enlightens his people lead to a convergence that translates the believer from this life into the life to come?

This truth is further confirmed by the life of one of the giants of biblical faith tradition who bears this same name. Enoch, the seventh generation from Adam, was actually called *Hanokh* in Hebrew, from the root *hanakh*. This unique man, *Hanokh*, was said to have "walked with God" and pleased God to such a degree that God took him,[16] translating him so that he would not experience death.[17] Apparently he was walking in such proximity to God that one day he stepped from one dimension of reality into another. Because the Hebrew for education, *hannukh*, is also from the root *hanakh*, Enoch could also called a "scientist," or better yet, "educated," trained in the ways of the Lord.

From the story of Enoch we learn the lesson that walking with God is synonymous with pleasing God.[18] Pleasing God is manifest in being educated in and keeping his commandments.[19] This is the process of *halachah*, the Jewish understanding of the way in which one should walk. It is a dedicated, progressive, ambulatory action, a walk with God in which there is no condemnation.[20] The narrowing or dedicating of the walk with God is the process of sanctification, the progressive work in which one submits to the washing of water by the Word of God[21] so that whatever lacks purity in his life is cleansed and separated unto God and his service. It is also the work of holiness which is an outgrowth of the righteousness that is imputed to the believer for his faith. Sanctification and holiness are essential to the process of walking with God.

Jesus demonstrated the fact that this kind of dedication to the purposes of God will bring forth divine illumination into the lives of humanity through the agency of such dedicated believers. In the introduction to the Sermon on the Mount, he outlined the beatitudes, the blessings he pronounced upon those who demonstrate the qualities of spirit that reflect godly character.[22] Immediately thereafter, he indicated that dedication to a lifestyle that manifests these qualities causes men to be the "light of the world." He urged his disciples to "let your light so shine before men, that they may see your good works, and glorify your Father in heaven."[23]

What brings light into the world is not the pronouncement of one's faith, the recitation of a litany of beliefs about ideas, concepts, and teachings. Light is manifest when one does the "good works" that are the outworking of one's faith in a godly lifestyle. It is not inherent in the human spirit to be self-sacrificing for the benefit of others. Selfishness is inherent in man because of sin. It is only when one is filled with the light of God's presence that he is illuminated and empowered to do the good works that will bring honor to the Eternal Father.

When one walks in the ever-narrowing path of righteousness, he finds himself fulfilling the only new commandment given in the New Testament: "A new commandment I give to you, that you love one another; even as I have loved you, that you also love one another."[24] This love transcends loving one's neighbor as himself. It demands that the believer love in the same manner and to the same degree with which Jesus loved the world. This love is manifest in the sacrifice of self and ambition in order to minister to the well-being of others. It is a very narrowing and restricting walk that can be achieved only through the dedication of sanctification and the empowerment of the Holy Spirit.

Is it any wonder, then, that such walking with God on the narrow path enlists the deployment of divine light on the believer's pathway? The act of dedication, of separating for God's service, always brings the light of inspiration and understanding into the life of the believer. As it did in the ancient time when the temple was cleansed and the lamp was lit, so dedication produces light both for Jews and Christians.

Ultimately when the Messiah comes, the final dedication will take place. Believers in the God of heaven and earth who have been resurrected to a newness of life through faith in the Messiah[25] will be resurrected to eternal life and clothed upon with immortality,[26] ever to live in the presence of God. Christians and Jews who have struggled throughout their lifetimes against the evil inclination to manifest in their lives the light of good works that bring glory to God will find themselves full of light. As the Jewish people have long expected, the Messianic Era will be the time for the "actualized potential for humanity."[27] All the potential with which man was endowed at his creation will be fully realized as the light of resurrection glory radiates through all men of faith, Jew and Gentile.

HANUKKAH AND THE MESSIANIC AGE

The story of Hanukkah is a perfect metaphor for the coming Messianic Age. The events of this time described in the two apocryphal books of Maccabees were predicted by the prophet Daniel while he was in Babylonian captivity. He warned of the coming of a dominant power (the "little horn") that would rise out of the Grecian empire, and he even predicted that the duration of its domination over Judah would be just under seven years.[28] Previously Daniel had also noted the duration of his reign of terror as being approximately three and one-half years.[29] He accurately predicted the actions of Antiochus Epiphanes in Israelite society from his initial policy of peace, to his subsequent acts of violence against the Jewish people, to his desecration of the temple (which lasted exactly three years), to his exalting himself against the Most High, to his own ultimate destruction "without human hand."[30] This account is amazing in the detailed accuracy with which it predicted the events that followed.

Couched in the language describing the historical Antiochus event, however, are statements that speak of the coming of the Messiah and the Messianic Age. Coupled with another vision,[31] God gave much detail through Daniel of the time preceding the Messiah. Jesus and the apostles, including Paul, drew much of their apocalyptic understanding from Daniel's prophecies. Jesus himself referred to Daniel's predictions when he answered the questions asked by his disciples about the timing of Jerusalem's impending destruction and the advent of the Messianic Era. Jesus warned his disciples, "So when you see the desolating sacrilege standing in the holy place, as was spoken of by the prophet Daniel . . . then those in Judea must flee to the mountains."[32] Paul spoke of deception by a policy of peace on the part of this world power: "While they are saying, 'Peace and safety!' then destruction will come upon them."[33] He concluded, however, by noting that the Son of man would return to the earth in such great power and glory that every eye will see him.[34]

Much later, Paul answered concerns in the church at Thessalonica about the coming of the Messiah and the gathering of the universal congregation of believers to him.[35] He predicted boldly that that day would not come until after the man of lawlessness, the son of perdition, had been revealed and after he had established himself as deity in the temple of God.[36] The only source for Paul's assertion is

Daniel's prophecies, where the blaspheming political power, the last in a line of empires (beginning with Babylon and continuing through Medo-Persia, Greece, and Rome) rises to bring violence to Israel and the "righteous ones." His conclusion is the same as Daniel's: this blasphemous world power will be destroyed without hand by the spirit of the Messiah's mouth and the brightness of his coming.[37]

Jesus and the earliest church, then, saw the events which are celebrated at Hanukkah as being predictive of the advent of the Messiah and the age of universal peace. The apostolic eschatology that was so prominent in the nascent church envisioned the rise of world political powers that would coalesce into one dominant figure, much like Antiochus Epiphanes, who would wreak havoc on Israel and the church. They expected this character ultimately to be a manifestation of Satan himself and the reign of terror that accompanied his dominion as being profoundly destructive to the earth and its inhabitants.

The Apocalypse of John gives graphic details of his vision of the eschaton. John's vision, however, is "the Revelation of Jesus Christ,"[38] not the revelation of demonic forces and world political domination. The centerpiece of his eschatological scenario is manifest when the Messiah comes, followed by the armies of heaven, to vanquish the evil one and his minions and to establish a millennium of peace.[39] This is the ultimate fulfillment of the messianic expectation that has been the focal point of faith for all biblical religion. It is the scarlet thread of hope that is woven throughout the fabric of Holy Scripture, from Genesis to Revelation. Both the first and the last promises in Scripture confirm this blessed hope.[40] For centuries, both Jews and Christians have awaited this event, Jews anticipating the *coming* of the Messiah, Christians expecting the *return* of the Messiah. Both view the Messiah's coming as the ultimate divine victory over evil and the establishing of universal peace and righteousness in the earth.

With all the abominations that are to be manifest in the time immediately prior to the coming of the Messiah and the accompanying persecution of the saints of God, the situation will exactly parallel that of the Maccabean conflict. This will be a time for the fulfillment of Zechariah's prophecy: "But I will camp around my house because of an army . . . and no oppressor will pass over them anymore . . . Rejoice greatly, O daughter of Zion! Shout in triumph, O daughter of Jerusalem! Behold, your king is coming to you; he is just and endowed with salvation, humble, and mounted on a donkey, even on a colt, the foal of a donkey. . . . Return to the stronghold, O prisoners who have the hope; this very day I am declaring that I will restore double to you. For I will bend Judah as my bow, I will fill the bow with Ephraim. And I will stir up your sons, O Zion, against your sons, O Greece . . . Then the Lord will appear over them, and his arrow will go forth like lightning; and the Lord God will blow the trumpet . . ."[41]

As in the days of the Maccabees when God's Spirit stirred up the sons of Zion against the sons of Greece and expelled the abominable Antiochus from the land, God will again stir up his people against neo-paganism (the revival of pagan mythologies), New Age philosophy (featuring concepts of Eastern monism, blended with neo-Platonism), and every other concept and political power that exalts itself against the knowledge of God. Both Judaism and Christianity will come alongside one another in cooperation to fight against this global threat both to biblical religion and to civilization itself, as God again raises up all the sons of Zion, both Jews and Christians, against the forces of Hellenism. At the height of the battle, the Lord, King Messiah, will appear over them, sending forth the lightning that stretches from one end of heaven to the other. He will blow the "last shofar," the great trumpet, that will awaken the dead unto the resurrection[42] and signal the initiation of the Messianic Age. That shofar, the last of seven, will speak these words: "The kingdom of the world has become the kingdom of our Lord and of his Christ, and he will reign for ever and ever."[43] The one who came in humility, mounted on the foal of a donkey,[44] will return in triumph, riding a white horse and followed by the armies of heaven.[45]

When the Messiah comes, it will be time for rededication, a Hanukkah to exceed all previous celebrations. Perhaps this will be the time when God will search Jerusalem with lamps,[46] punishing the complacent and purifying the world's capital city. *Ha satan*, the archenemy of the righteous, will be bound and cast into the abyss,[47] freeing humanity from temptations by his angels. King Messiah will be enthroned, and a restoration and rededication process will ensue in which the entire planet will be renewed–politically, economically, ecologically, religiously, and in every other possible way.[48]

The menorah will be lit with the pure, consecrated oil of the Holy Spirit, and the light of God will shine as never before in human history as God himself will be the light of the world. Isaiah predicted this light: "The sun will no more be your light by day, nor will the brightness of the moon shine on you, for the Lord will be your everlasting light, and your God will be your glory."[49] This theme is echoed in John's apocalyptic words: "And the city has no need of sun or moon to shine on it, for the glory of God is its light, and its lamp is the Lamb."[50] God and the Lamb are the menorah of the new Jerusalem.

The Messiah himself will be the light of the renovated earth. He who was light from the beginning of creation will be the only light of the redeemed. The Living Menorah will radiate the glory of his eternal presence into the lives of all the righteous who have ever lived, both Jews and Gentiles. The radiance will be unfathomable and indescribable. Isaiah spoke of the intensity of this light: "The light of the moon will be as the light of the sun, and the light of the sun will be seven times brighter, like the light of seven days, on the day the Lord binds up the fracture of his people and heals the bruise he has inflicted."[51] One commentary suggests that because Israel made the menorah for God, God will make it shine on Israel "sevenfold in the Messianic Age."[52] The miracle of Hanukkah will be renewed, only this time, the light will be multiplied seven times in intensity. Just as the light burned for seven additional days on a one-day supply of oil in antiquity, so the light of the living Menorah, the Messiah himself, will shine with such brilliance that a sevenfold light will shine each day. The seven flames of fire before the throne of God in heaven will be manifest in the earth as the seven spirits of God run to and fro throughout all the earth,[53] radiating the glory of God's presence so that his knowledge will cover the earth as the waters cover the sea.[54]

What a profound event! What a glorious time! "God, who commanded the light to shine out of darkness," who has shined "in our hearts, to give the light of the knowledge of the glory of God in the face of Jesus Christ"[55] will radiate his glory into all the earth through his only begotten Son, "the brightness of his glory, and the express image of his person."[56] God will be supreme, and man will experience the intensity of the divine light that has enshrouded the Eternal from eternity past. God's Lamp will fully become man's light!

[1] These included injunctions against idolatry, murder, and adultery.

[2] Rudolph Brasch, *The Judaic Heritage* (New York: David McKay Co., 1969), p. 315.

[3] Babylonian Talmud, *Rosh Ha-Shanah 24b, 'Avodah Zarah 43a.*

[4] Daniel Sperber, "The History of the Menorah," *Journal of Jewish Studies*, XVI, Nos. 3, 4, 1965, p. 138.

[5] *Ibid.*, p. 142.

[6] Lewis Ginsberg, *Legends of the Jews* (1946), 3, p. 166.

[7] Babylonian Talmud. *Shabbat* 21b. *Megillath Ta'anith*, chapter 9.

[8] O. S. Rankin, *The Origins of the Festival of Hanukkah* (Edinburg: T. T. Clark, 1930), p. 93.

[9] 1 Maccabees 4:50-52.

[10] See the Website: *www.acs.calgary.ca/~elsegal/shokel/951215_menorah.html*
[11] John 10:22, 23.
[12] Rudolph Brasch, p. 318.
[13] Matthew 7:14.
[14] John 17:17.
[15] Psalm 43:3, New International Version.
[16] Genesis 5:24.
[17] Hebrews 11:5.
[18] Genesis 5:22; Hebrews 11:5.
[19] Isaiah 42:21; John 14:15.
[20] Romans 8:1.
[21] Ephesians 5:26.
[22] Matthew 5:1-13.
[23] Matthew 5:16.
[24] John 13:34, Revised Standard Version.
[25] Romans 6:4.
[26] 2 Corinthians 5:4.
[27] See the Website: *www.ou.org/chagim/chanukah/machloket.htm*
[28] Daniel 8:9-14.
[29] Daniel 7:25.
[30] Daniel 8:25.
[31] Daniel 7:1-28.
[32] Matthew 24:15, New Revised Standard Version.
[33] 1 Thessalonians 5:3, New American Standard Version.
[34] Revelation 1:7.
[35] 2 Thessalonians 2:1-4.
[36] 2 Thessalonians 2:1-3.
[37] 2 Thessalonians 2:8.
[38] Revelation 1:1-2.
[30] Revelation 19:11-21.
[40] Genesis 3:15; Revelation 22:20.
[41] Zechariah 9:8-14, New American Standard Version.
[42] 1 Corinthians 15:52.
[43] Revelation 11:15, New International Version.
[44] Matthew 21:5.
[45] Revelation 19:11.
[46] Zephaniah 1:12, New International Version.
[47] Revelation 20:1-3.
[48] Acts 3:20-21.
[49] Isaiah 60:19, New International Version.
[50] Revelation 21:23, New Revised Standard Version.
[51] Isaiah 30:26, New American Standard Version.
[52] *Midrash Rabbah*, Exodus 50:4.
[53] Zechariah 4:10.
[54] Isaiah 11:9.
[55] 2 Corinthians 4:6.
[56] Hebrews 1:3.

Chapter 16

Synagogue and Church Aflame

At the depth of night when darkness is pervasive, the menorah should be burning its brightest. Likewise, when the world is at its darkest hour, the light of God's chosen people, both Israel and the church, should be burning most intensely. This is why Paul underscored the fact that believers were to shine as "lights in the world" in the midst of a wicked and perverse nation.[1] Each believer is to be a "mini-menorah," as it were. Unfortunately, the opposite is too frequently true. When evil has vaunted itself in history, believers, both Jews and Christians, have often lacked the fortitude to stand up and speak out.

BEFORE THE LAMP IS EXTINGUISHED

A good example of this was found in the time of Eli and Samuel.[2] Because Eli the priest chose to ignore the immorality of his own sons in the very confines of the sanctuary itself, bad times befell Israel. As a result of this spiritual decline, there was "no open vision" and the Word of God was "rare in those days."[3] Immorality–even amorality–in leadership always precludes the revelation for the insight into God's Word that gives vision and purpose to God's people. When vision is absent, people cast off restraint.[4] When the Spirit of revelation is not manifest, the letter of the Word fails to produce light.[5]

At the lowest point of Eli's leadership, these classic words revealed Israel's condition and God's resolve to bring his people to renewal and restoration: "Before the lamp of God went out in the tabernacle of the Lord where the ark of God was . . . the Lord called Samuel. And he answered, 'Here I am!' "[6] Often the lamp of God is on the verge of being extinguished in the earth because of the ignorance, apathy, or downright rebellion of God's people; however, God always summons a prophetic voice of insight and resolve who will issue the shofar's clarion call to bring God's people to repentance and renewal. This was the case with Samuel, the prophet whose words never fell to the ground.[7]

Because of Israel's disobedience, they were soundly defeated in battle by the Philistines. Then someone came up with the brilliant idea that what they needed to assure victory was to take the ark of the covenant into battle. The reputation of the ark gave them a sense of security, for in it were artifacts that spoke of God's commitment to Israel.[8] The tablets of the law symbolized God's covenant with Israel. Aaron's rod confirmed the fact that Israel had the right of access to God through the priesthood. The pot of manna revealed that there would never be an occasion when God would not provide for them. The Israelites, therefore had every reason to believe that the ark's presence in battle would ensure their victory. When the next battle ensued, however, Israel suffered an even more staggering defeat, and the ark which they had trusted was captured by their enemies.[9] Then they finally realized that the glory of God had departed.[10] Later Samuel led Israel in repentance, and the people returned to God. Subsequently, God thundered his approval, and so confused the enemy that they were overcome by Israel.

This scenario reveals the fact that mere religiosity is insufficient for victory. Even God's own system is merely a box of relics if the *Shekhinah* is not present. The most important element in the Holy of Holies was not the ark or the cherubim. It was God's manifest presence, the *Shekhinah.* It is God's Spirit, not man's religiosity, that brings victory.

There is a clear parallel between this biblical story and the history and present condition of the Christian church. Like Israel, the church lost the vision of its unique calling to be the light of the world, a city set on a hill that cannot be hidden.[11] In history, the fire of the Holy Spirit that illuminated the Gentile world through the teaching of the apostles slowly dimmed and was finally extinguished by the introduction of pagan concepts and practices into the church's teaching and polity. The result was the Dark Ages, so called because of the abysmal apostasy of the church and the profound ignorance and superstition of the people under its aegis. The light of the menorah was reduced to a flicker, a testimony to the power that darkness can exercise over amoral leaders and perverted ecclesiastical systems.

REMOVE THE LAMPSTAND?

Sadly, much of the Christian church both in history and today deserves the same indictment that the angel gave the church at Ephesus. The people and the bureaucracies that they have maintained and still maintain have departed from the church's first love. God's judgment in Ephesus was this: "I will . . . remove your lampstand."[12] The menorah was obviously still a symbol of import to the congregations of the Christian church, even in its Gentile communities. This example suggests that a menorah symbol was displayed even among Gentile Judaeo-Christian congregations in Asia Minor years after Jesus' ascension. The menorah may well have served as a visible symbol of the life and light of the church. At any rate, the angel's ultimatum was clear and final: Restore your first love and passion for God, or suffer the loss of the lampstand.

The condition of the Ephesian church was somewhat parallel with that at Laodicea. Though the church there considered itself successful, wealthy, increased with goods, and lacking nothing, God declared that it was poor, wretched, miserable, and blind.[13] He was primarily troubled with the lukewarm condition of the Laodicean congregation that had long since lost its passion for God and his Word. Concerned with materialism, the Laodiceans believed that godliness was confirmed by gain.[14] What were they thinking? Had not Jesus clearly stated, "You cannot serve God and mammon"?[15] The Laodiceans were suffering from a vision problem. They had turned from the light of the menorah and had embraced other interests. They were instructed to anoint their eyes with eye salve so that once again they would have vision and insight into the purposes of God.

Too many congregations, both Christians and Jews, are more concerned for the material than the spiritual. They focus on maintaining the *status quo*, the unrelenting quest for survival of bureaucracies. They lack passion. They fail to revere God and his Word. They lack the fundamental understanding that the fear of God is the beginning of wisdom.[16] Yet, in their wealthy status, they are impoverished, having exchanged the jewels of divine revelation for the baubles of human traditions, the priceless gold of divine anointing for the iron pyrite of lifeless ritual.

Many congregations, both Christian and Jewish, are lacking in illumination. Though eternal flames may be burning in their sanctuaries and synagogues, these people are so lacking in passion for God and his eternal truth that they at times seem to stand at the very brink of accommodating almost anything. If there was ever a burning menorah in these congregations, its flames have long since been extinguished. Perhaps God is issuing the same ultimatum to these brass *objets d'art*: Come alive in the Holy Spirit and let the light of the

Word shine, or the menorah will be utterly removed.

In order to avoid this tragic judgment, the synagogue and the church must return to its first love, its passion for God. The greatest of all the commandments declared, "You shall love the Lord your God with all your heart, and with all your soul, and with all your mind, and with all your strength."[17] The one sure thing that will cause the menorah to be extinguished and eventually to be removed is the loss of this first love.

TRIMMED AND BURNING

This is why it is essential that the light be accorded the greatest reverence and diligence. Daily attendance to the light–keeping the lamp trimmed and burning–is the duty of dedicated believers both individually and collectively. God's lamp does not automatically shine its light in man, through man, to man. Illumination takes work and dedication in partnership with God.

The lighting of the menorah's lamps in Israel's sanctuaries gives us insight into the requirements for raising the light. The daily exercise was a carefully orchestrated function of the temple priesthood. In the wilderness tabernacle, the lamps of the newly constructed menorah were cleaned by the priests in the morning and lit in the evening with the consecrated fire from the altar. This offered a vivid contrast between man's spiritual needs (light) and his material needs (bread). It also demonstrated that the very Word of God (the bread of life) can be ingested and give sustenance to the human soul only when it is illuminated by the light of the Eternal. Later tradition says that the center lamp of the menorah burned continuously, both day and night, and from it the additional lamps were lit in the evening.

The menorah stood on the south wall of the temple sanctuary opposite the table of showbread; therefore, its lamps were arranged from east to west. It is said that the lamp atop the central shaft of the menorah was turned in a westerly direction, facing the *Shekhinah* on the mercy seat of the ark of the covenant.[18] The six outer lamps were oriented in such a way that their light was cast in the direction of the center lamp.

The central lamp's continual flame motif is so important that the *ner tamid* of a new synagogue is usually lit with the fire from the perpetual light of an older synagogue.[19] This everlasting light that originated in the menorah's central lamp is a symbol of the ever-present God of whom it is said, "He who keeps Israel will neither slumber nor sleep."[20] It also is a demonstration of uninterrupted worship on earth that parallels that which is practiced in heaven where the angelic hosts never cease exclaiming, "Holy, holy, holy, is the Lord God Almighty, who was, and is, and is to come."[21]

The fact that the menorah required cleaning and relighting demonstrates graphically that if God's lamp is to remain man's light in the earth, the kingdom of priests unto God (all believers) must be dedicated to the process of cleaning and removing the remains of yesterday's light and rekindling the flames afresh each day. Far too often, when divine insight is given, people begin to systematize and memorialize and even worship that light rather than honor and walk in it, all the while looking forward toward the further unfolding of the light for a new day. For the light to be perpetual, the menorah must be cleaned, trimmed, and relit daily.

This truth also underscores the fact that eternal vigilance is necessary for the continued advancement of God's truth. The written Word of God of itself is not a perpetual lamp that unceasingly radiates a beacon of hope. A world in darkness cannot hear the Word of light unless it is preached.[22] God truly is in partnership with his chosen people to raise the light and radiate it into the world.

RAISING THE LIGHT

In spite of widespread apostasy, a large number of believers who are biblicists stand squarely and unequivocally for the divine truth that is represented in the Word of God. In some cases, Jews outshine Christians when it comes to upholding biblical morality and ethics. One only need cite the example of the Jewish students who challenged the requirements of former "Christian" universities like Yale that forced them to live in dormitories where fornication and other sexual immorality were encouraged by the system and flaunted by their fellow students. There is also the case of the young Jewish girl who was so affronted by the lack of modesty at formerly "Christian" Princeton that she created a media frenzy by insisting that modesty is preferable to outright lasciviousness.

On the other hand, there are millions of Christians in thousands of congregations around the world who have been labeled extremists by the secular media because they insist on believing and practicing the absolute ethics of the Ten Commandments rather than participating in the situational ethics of consequentialism that have been promoted by an increasingly hostile, humanistic society and its governmental agencies. When evil abounds, grace is much more abundant.[23] When darkness is at its thickest and most pervasive, light radiates forth as a beacon of hope to the lost and dying. Even the smallest flickering candle is enlightening in abject darkness. The age-old confrontation between the sons of light and the sons of darkness that so captivated the imagination of the Qumran community of first-century Israel is growing larger and larger.

Part of the strategy of the realm of darkness is an attempt to substitute darkness for light, bitter for sweet, and evil for good. Such was the lamentation of Isaiah: "Woe unto them that call evil good, and good evil; that put darkness for light, and light for darkness; that put bitter for sweet, and sweet for bitter!"[24] What is patently evil is championed as good, for liberated modern men and women think they must be free to do anything that their hearts imagine. But an even greater evil follows the same path as in Isaiah's day: "[They] justify the wicked for reward, and take away the righteousness of the righteous from him!"[25] The right conduct spelled out in God's Word is so disparaged that many begin to question it and eventually have it taken away from them by the challenges of evil and by their own fears of being ostracized as nonconformists.

Throughout history, however, millions of Jews and Christians have faced such challenges, refusing to compromise with the darkness that causes light to be extinguished. Their fiery passion for the Eternal cannot be quenched by even the most pervasive darkness and wickedness. They become living firebrands of the good news that God's kingdom ultimately will fully triumph over all evil. Like Samson's foxes, they set the enemy's fields on fire.[26] These are the living menorahs, the living emblems of truth and righteousness. God's lamps they are, shining forth man's light into a world of darkness.

Daniel was one such shining light. Forced into slavery in Babylon, he rose to political power by the purity of his heart that radiated forth God's light. He made a public demonstration of praying three times daily. He graciously excused himself from eating the king's foods. He and his colleagues refused to bow to Nebuchadnezzar's golden image. And, he alone in the world's most powerful kingdom was able to translate the message written on the wall of the Babylonian palace by the hand of God. Interestingly enough, this encrypted message was written on the wall "beside the candlestick,"[27] which could well have been the menorah that Nebuchadnezzar had taken as part of the spoils from conquered Jerusalem. This incident occurred during a royal banquet in which the "gold vessels that had been taken out of the temple, the house of God which was in Jerusalem" were brought forth and used by the Babylonians. What if God's words of judgment upon Belshazzar's regime were emblazoned beside the menorah as a testimony to the fact that God will always judge those who impede the advance of his light?

Near the end of Daniel's career, he declared that "those who have insight will shine brightly like the brightness of the expanse of heaven, and those who lead the many to righteousness, like the stars forever and ever."[28] The wise of the earth are those who allow the light of God to shine in their lives so that they direct those around them to the path of righteousness. The reward for their being such inspiring channels of illumination will be their positions as luminaries through the endless ages of eternity.

DISPLAYING THE SYMBOL OF LIGHT

Because the post-Second-Temple rabbis forbade the construction of menorahs with seven branches,[29] Rabbinic Judaism substituted the "eternal flame" for the menorah in synagogues. While this long-standing tradition in Judaism does not permit the use of the menorah in synagogues, there is no biblical prohibition regarding its use as a symbol and implement of faith. The fact that Solomon contracted with Hiram of Tyre to construct ten golden menorahs and placed five on both sides of the biblical menorah at the entrance leading to the Holy of Holies[30] is evidence that copies or models have been used in history and may be legitimately employed today.

According to a strong Jewish tradition, the image displayed on King David's shield was not, as many have assumed, a six-pointed star (the so-called Magen David) but a menorah inscribed with these words: "May God be gracious to us, and bless us and make his face to shine upon us."[31] The menorah was likely the shield of David as well as the seal of Solomon.[32] *The Golden Menorah*, published in Prague in the sixteenth century, declared, "This psalm, together with the menorah, is an allusion to great things. . . King David used to bear this psalm inscribed, pictured, and engraved on his shield, on a sheet of gold, in the shape of the menorah, when he went forth to battle, and he would meditate on its mystery, and conquer."[33] Perhaps if more Christians and Jews prominently displayed the menorah either in graphic or sculpted form, their meditation on God's lamp would bring illumination to their lives and help them conquer fear and temptation. Because the menorah is a living emblem that speaks loudly of God's enlightenment for man, it deserves prominent iconographic display.

A parade of history's tyrants has sought to destroy the menorah. First, Nebuchadnezzar may have taken the temple menorah along with other vessels when he looted Solomon's temple. Then, Antiochus Epiphanes destroyed the menorah in his attempt to replace the light of monotheism with Hellenism. The Maccabean menorah was likely made of some inferior material; however, the religious significance of that menorah was perhaps even greater than its predecessors, considering the miracle of light that occurred at its dedication (*hanukkah*). Later, in Herod's grandiose attempt to supersede the splendor of Solomon's temple, he constructed a new and glorious solid-gold menorah, said to be over four feet in height and three feet in width, with branches four inches thick. This menorah was probably part of the spoils of war that Titus deposited in Rome's Temple of Peace. When the vandals subsequently plundered Rome, they carried the menorah to Carthage only to have it removed to Byzantium by Justinian. A Jew there convinced Justinian that the menorah should be returned to Palestine where it was kept in the custody of the Christian community. When the Persians later captured Jerusalem in the seventh century, they plundered the Christian sanctuaries. Since that time, there is no information as to the menorah's whereabouts. Legends suggest that it was secreted away by holy men, much as tradition purports that the original temple menorah was hidden, perhaps by Jeremiah, before Nebuchadnezzar's invasion.

It may well be that both temporal and spiritual principalities and powers have sought to deny believers the use of history's greatest living emblem. It is the piety of the Jewish sages who insisted that nothing originally standing in the temple could be reproduced until it is needed for the Third Temple that has militated against the more frequent and open use of this living emblem. That it was a strong symbol in synagogues of Jesus' time is clear from his own reference to the light of the world on a candlestick[34] and from the Apocalypse's imagery, both in the view of the glorified Messiah and in the positioning of the "lampstand" in the Ephesian church.[35]

Since each home is to be a *mikdash me'at* (mini-sanctuary), it would seem quite appropriate that believers should have a menorah in their homes to symbolize the divine light of the sanctuary. This living emblem would offer great spiritual insight and object lessons for home devotion and study. The menorah should be more than a mantelpiece decoration, however. It should be an honored symbol, a material demonstration of Jesus the Messiah as the light of the world.

Many churches use candelabra of various sorts during ceremonies and worship, and these are certainly legitimate visual displays. The menorah, however, is a living emblem of profound and continuing significance to Christians. While the ancient menorah has been lost in antiquity, the emblem remains viable. The menorah is certainly appropriate for use in the sanctuaries of all communions today. This is an excellent way to demonstrate the continuity

of the church with the ancient congregation of God among
the Jews. It is also a means of clearly manifesting the roots
of Christian faith in biblical and Second Temple Judaism.
If the lighting of the lamps in the tent of meeting and in all
subsequent sanctuaries of Judaism was appropriate in demonstrating the Divine Presence among God's chosen people,
then it certainly should remain so today. After all, "Jesus
Christ [is] the same, yesterday, and today, and forever."[36]
God simply does not change; therefore, he continues to
require what he has expected of his people. One of his de-
sires is to see his people raise his light upon his lamp.

TIME FOR RESTORATION

Now, in this era of restoration and preparation for the
Messianic Age, is it not time for both Jewish and Christian
communities to rise up and relight the menorah, bringing
forth the radiance of God's lamp (his Word) to be man's
light? In this time when iniquity abounds and the love of
many has consequently grown cold (Matthew 24:12), are
blazing menorahs not needed to illuminate human path-
ways? As Christians and Jews share together in the display
of the material representations of God's lamp, may both
communities be man's light, illuminating the world with
the Divine Presence.

The eternal God is restless and will remain so, watching over his chosen people "till [their] righteousness goes
forth as brightness, and [their] salvation as a lamp that
burns."[37] Both Israel and the church are God's lamp of salvation glistening in the darkness of a world of sin. God
will see to it that both Israel and the church are manifesta-
tions of his lamp, man's light.

[1] Philippians 2:15.
[2] 1 Samuel 3.
[3] 1 Samuel 3:1, New King James Version.
[4] Proverbs 29:18.

[5] 2 Corinthians 3:6.

[6] 1 Samuel 3:3-4.

[7] 1 Samuel 3:19.

[8] Hebrews 9:4.

[9] 1 Samuel 4:11.

[10] 1 Samuel 4:21.

[11] Matthew 5:14.

[12] Revelation 2:5, New International Version.

[13] Revelation 3:17.

[14] 1 Timothy 6:5.

[15] Matthew 6:24.

[16] Psalm 111:10.

[17] Mark 12:30.

[18] Erwin R. Goodenough, *Jewish Symbols in the Greco-Roman Period* (New York: Pantheon Books, 1954), p.88.

[19] L. Yarden, *The Tree of Light* (Ithaca, New York: Cornell University Press, 1971), p. 13.

[20] Psalm 121:4, New Revised Standard Version.

[21] Revelation 4:8.

[22] Romans 10:15.

[23] Romans 5:20.

[24] Isaiah 5:20, King James Version.

[25] Isaiah 5:23, King James Version.

[26] Judges 15:4.

[27] Daniel 5:5.

[28] Daniel 12:3.

[29] Babylonian Talmud, *Rosh Hashanah* 24a-b; *Avodah Zarah* 43a; *Menahot* 28b.

[30] Nathan Ausubel, *The Book of Jewish Knowledge* (New York: Crown Publishers, 1964), p. 276.

[31] Psalm 67:1.

[32] Gershom Sholem, "The Curious History of the Six-pointed Star," *Commentary*, VIII (1949), p. 248.

[33] Quoted in L. Yarden, *The Tree of Light* (Ithaca, New York: Cornell University Press, 1971), p. v.

[34] Matthew 5:14.

[35] Revelation 2:5.

[36] Hebrews 13:8.

[37] Isaiah 62:1, New King James Version.

Index

Restoration Foundation
P. O. Box 421218
Atlanta, GA 30342